THE SOUTHWEST INSIDE OUT

AN ILLUSTRATED GUIDE TO THE LAND AND ITS HISTORY

The Southwest
INSIDEOUT

TEXT BY THOMAS WIEWANDT AND MAUREEN WILKS

PHOTOGRAPHY BY THOMAS WIEWANDT

DESIGN BY CAROL HARALSON

WILD HORIZONS PUBLISHING / TUCSON

Second Edition 2004   10 9 8 7 6 5 4

Printed in China

ISBN 1-879728-04-4

Publisher's Cataloging-in-Publication Data:

Wiewandt, Thomas A. (Thomas Alan)

  The Southwest - inside out : an illustrated guide to the land and its
history / text by Thomas Wiewandt and Maureen Wilks ; photography by
Thomas Wiewandt ; design by Carol Haralson - 2nd ed.

p. cm.

Includes bibliographical references and index.

1. Natural history — Southwest, New — Pictorial works.

2. Desert — Southwest, New — Pictorial works.

3. Geology — Southwest, New — Pictorial works.

4. Desert ecology — Southwest, New — Pictorial works.

I. Wilks, Maureen. II. Title.

QH104.5.S6 W54 2004

508.79 Library of Congress Control Number: 2003098300

Wild Horizons Publishing

P. O. Box 5118

Tucson, Arizona 85703-0118 U.S.A.

Tel. 520-743-4551; Fax. 520-743-4552

Website Contact: http://www.wildhorizons.com

This book is available at discounted prices for bulk purchases
in the United States by corporations, institutions, and other
organizations.

WHEREVER ONE GOES IN THE
SOUTHWEST ONE ENCOUNTERS MAGIC,
STRENGTH, AND BEAUTY. MYRIAD
MIRACLES IN TIME AND PLACE OCCUR;
THERE IS NO END TO THE GRANDEURS
AND INTIMACIES, NO END TO THE
REVIVAL OF THE SPIRIT WHICH THEY
OFFER TO ALL. — ANSEL ADAMS

THIS BOOK IS DEDICATED TO
DAVID MORTON, WHO BELIEVES IN
THAT MAGIC, AND IN THOSE MIRACLES.

Contents

THIS BOOK CELEBRATES heroic landscapes of the American Southwest—what they are, where they are, and how they came to be. It's part travel guide, part primer, part resource directory. And it's also a photographic portfolio drawn from 15 years of work. The content is written and organized so that it can be opened anywhere and easily absorbed by anyone intrigued by the diverse and astounding scenery of the Southwest.

So get ready to travel and to dive beneath the surface of what meets the eye. This means time travel as well as the on-the-road kind. We've endeavored to bring to life a few pages from the history of our planet, an exciting but incomplete record distilled from centuries of scientific inquiry. Come equipped with an active imagination and a certain amount of faith. Who among us, after all, can comprehend the enormity of a million years? A billion? In the well-chosen words of Carl Sagan, "We are like butterflies who flutter for a day and think it is forever."

Before embarking on this journey, we ask that you consider three things. First, be aware that no scene before you is a finished masterpiece of nature—there is no such thing. While Utah's Delicate Arch, for example, might seem fixed, perfected, and going nowhere, the entire landscape is changing today, just as it always has been. The secret is time, nothing more.

Second, our emphasis here is on *process,* not place. We want you to discover the excitement of things that many people pass by. This book will guide you to notable scenic attractions in the American Southwest; but look beyond our examples, beyond designated *picture stops.* Our biggest reward would come from knowing that those who read this book will be able to see and appreciate unannounced features of the land that would otherwise have gone unnoticed.

Third, the territory we cover might come as a surprise. By Southwest, we mean the Greater Southwest, defined more by natural features of desert and canyon country than by political boundaries. Our geographic range extends from northern Mexico to the northern limits of the Colorado Plateau in Utah and Colorado. It runs from California's eastern slopes of the Sierra Nevada across the states of Nevada, Arizona, and New Mexico, into western Texas. And where it makes sense, we took the liberty of reaching a little beyond these limits. We also chose to restrict our coverage to landscapes evident above ground—delving into caves could fill another volume.

You'll discover more than geology in these pages. Because rocks shape the ways of living creatures and living creatures in turn shape rocks—both at the mercy of outside forces—we've created a blend of all three. If you wish to dig deeper, flip to our annotated listings in the back, where you'll find a wealth of stimulating books and websites. For travelers, we have assembled seven regional maps, along with an extensive list of scenic attractions packed with earthly wonders.

Enjoy the journey!

ACKNOWLEDGMENTS

Because of the broad geographic and editorial scope of this book and our intent to make it accurate but non-technical, many creative and scholarly individuals were vital to its development. Diana Turner helped to formulate the character of the project; and two writers, both with scientific expertise and a way with words—Susan Cummins Miller and Mari Jensen—made valuable contributions to portions of the text. Bob MacLeod, David Morton, and Elizabeth Shaw read much of the manuscript and offered helpful suggestions through-out. Sally Antrobus and Linda Gregonis edited the complete text with care, sensitivity, and professionalism found only in the best of editors. We also appreciate the authors and their publishers whose quoted words of wisdom and inspiration have enhanced our text. Thank you all.

The following 21 experts in their fields, mostly within the National Park Service, checked our text as a whole or in part for accuracy and clarity. We are extremely grateful for their enthusiastic and valuable responses—without exception, these friendly and dedicated individuals helped to make this a better book.

Arvid Aase/Fossil Butte National Monument; Sidney Ash, Paleobotanist; Terry Baldino, *Assistant Chief of Interpretation*/Death Valley National Park; John Bezy, *Staff Ranger*/Saguaro National Park; Anna Domitrovic, *Mineralogist & Collection Manager*/Arizona-Sonora Desert Museum; Stephanie Dubois, *Superintendent*/Chaco Culture National Historical Park; Tom Haraden, *Assistant Chief Naturalist*/Zion National Park; Paul Henderson, *Chief of Interpretation*/Canyonlands National Park; Wilson Hunter, *Chief of Interpretation*/Canyon de Chelly National Monument; Carol Kruse, *Interpretive Specialist*/Sunset Crater Volcano National Monument; John Mangimeli, *Chief Interpretive Ranger*/White Sands National Monument; Will Morris, former *Chief of Interpretation*/Mesa Verde National Park; Thea Nordling, former *Chief of Interpretation*/Capitol Reef National Park; Wanda Olszewski, *Interpretive Specialist*/Hueco Tanks State Historical Park; Steve Roof, *Assistant Professor* in Earth & Environmental Science/Hampshire College; Steve Sandell, *Chief Ranger*/Montezuma Castle National Monument; Tessy Shirakawa, *Chief of Interpretation*/Mesa Verde National Park; Harry Walters, *Director,* Hatathli Museum/Dineh College; David Whitman, *Chief of Interpretation*/Dinosaur National Monument; Justin Wilkinson, NASA Geomorphologist; James Woolsey, *Chief of Resource Interpretation*/Mojave National Preserve.

The importance of illustrators and designers in particular often goes unnoticed, but for a book to be inviting, lively, and easy to read, great design is crucial. Carol Haralson has worked wonders with this material, both as a talented designer and as an editor—thank you, Carol! And for the many fine maps and illustrations that embellish our text, we are pro-foundly grateful to David Fischer, Michael Robinson, Paul Mirocha, Leo Gabaldon, dinosaur sculptor John Fischner, Ray Sterner/Johns Hopkins University, and the team at Eureka Cartography in Berkeley. And we thank the photographers, government agencies, and corporations who provided images to extend our coverage—credits appear with each.

We wish to thank the following individuals, companies, and institutions for loans of the many superb specimens featured in these pages: John Alcorn; Arizona Historical Society; Arizona-Sonora Desert Museum; Arizona State Museum; Bill Hawes' Fossils; Black Hills Institute of Geological Research; Clare's Fossil Quarry; Simon Cohen Fossils; Susan Cummins Miller; Den's Petrified Critters; Jim Work/Dominican Amber Co.; Jimmy Vacek/Forty-Niner Minerals; Gem City, Laramie, Wyoming; Geological Enterprises; Thomas Johnson/House of Phacops; Jerry MacDonald/Paleozoic Trackways Project; David Morton; Phelps Dodge Corporation; Potomac Museum Group; Tucson Marble & Granite Co.; Rick Hebdon & Gael Summer/Warfield Fossils; Klaus Westphal/University of Wisconsin's Museum of Geology; and Richard White/International Wildlife Museum.

A note of gratitude is also due Wild Horizons photographic workshop participants who, over a decade of stimulating conversation and exploration in the Southwest, provided the catalyst for this book. Many other friends and colleagues contributed to the project in small-er but significant ways, and we genuinely appreciate your support and good faith as well.

M O R E than anything else, photography is about light; and in the clear, dry air so typical of the Southwest, the light is harsher than most people realize. Travelers from more humid places who have never photographed in the Southwest often return home surprised and disappointed by the results. Film is not as sensitive as the human eye, and it cannot record the full range of values from bright light to deep shadows (print film is a bit more forgiving than slide film). We need to work with these limitations, and the following tips are intended to help any photographer capture the beauty that abounds here.

P L A N N I N G *when* to shoot can be as important as where. Sunlight is weaker and warmer (redder) early and late in the day, and these are also the times when low, slanting light reveals textures often not evident during the midday hours (see cover). Because the sun never climbs high in the sky during winter months, winter light is often more favorable than summer light. And if you want to accentuate the red in red rock country, shoot when it's bathed in the warm rays of the rising or setting sun.

C A N Y O N S are often immersed in deep shade early and late in the day. But you can achieve satisfying results at any time by paying close attention to the light. Watch for opportunities to shoot when sunlight is skimming across a cliff face, accentuating textures (see p. 75). You may discover places where the bright, harsh light bounces off one canyon wall to illuminate the opposite wall in a soft glow that will register beautifully on film. Slot canyons, for example (see pp. 102-103), come to life at midday, but beware of "hot spots," patches of direct sunlight that will translate into distracting, bright blotches in photographs.

C L O U D S are among the Southwest's greatest blessings. Here, big sky meets grandiose landscape, and at times you'll want to compose images to emphasize sky. But apart from their beauty, as clouds float by they throw portions of the landscape into shade and other areas into dramatic, theatrical light. Be patient and watch carefully—with a little luck, the area of greatest interest will fall into a natural spotlight while its background remains in shadow (see p. 61).

Sometimes, as the sun peeks through the thin edge of a cloud, it casts soft light on your subject—perfect, low-contrast light for most film (see p. 133); you'll need to be attentive and quick to take advantage of these fleeting opportunities. Today's color-saturated films yield richer colors than you might expect in these situations. Similarly, be thankful for those rare days under thin overcast—the perfect time to pursue close-ups and tightly composed scenics that exclude the white sky (see pp. 138-139).

CONTROLLING THE LIGHT is still possible even when nature refuses to lend you a hand. Try a few tricks of the trade to soften harsh highlights and shadows outdoors, especially for close-ups. If your friend's face, for example, is lost in deep shadow below the brim of a hat, ask your companion to move to the shade. If your camera takes filters, you may want to add an 81B warming filter—film sees more blue light than normal in the shade. You can also try using a flash to fill the shadow with light. If the outcome proves too brightly lit, next time try covering the flash head with a diffuser, like a handkerchief. Or change settings on the flash unit to reduce the light output if your camera allows this.

Another helpful trick is to carry a thin collapsible light diffuser or a reflector. I prefer the convenience of those made by PhotoFlex—a circular diffuser 32" in diameter folds neatly into a 12" disk. The diffuser does a nice job softening light on flowers and other small objects (see p. 141), and the reflector works well to bounce light into deep shadows.

STORMS are opportunities. Travelers often pack up the camera when heavy clouds roll in—a mistake. Your eye may not find the scene especially appealing, but your photographs may profit from the soft light (see pp. 120-121). Go ahead, shoot it; and you may be pleasantly surprised. I can't begin to tell you how many times people spotting my camera and tripod have said, "You should have been here half an hour ago when the sun was out." I smile and think, "No, this is just what I need."

Desert storms add drama and excitement to photographs (see pp. 94-95). As my University of Arizona scientific illustration professor Donald Sayner used to say, "When it rains, shoot rainy-day pictures." Wonderful advice (see pp. 92-93). And when it rains, the unexpected often happens. A few years ago, one of my tour groups was caught in a downpour while riding in the back of an open truck on the floor of Canyon de Chelly. Within minutes, waterfalls appeared from nowhere, pouring over the scenic cliff faces, a bone-chilling experience but also the photographic opportunity of a lifetime (see pp. 66-67).

To capture lightning on film requires both art and science. Because small, active storm cells and good visibility typify the summer monsoon season in the desert Southwest, it's an ideal place to photograph lightning. Here are a few highlights to help you get started.

Because slow shutter speeds increase the probability of catching a strike while the shutter is open, you will need a camera support such as a bean bag or tripod. You should also have a telephoto lens to allow you to work at safe distances from the storm. Most cloud-to-ground lightning flashes pack more than one stroke—giving the strike a flickering appearance—and if you trip the shutter the instant you see the first stroke, you can sometimes catch the second or third one. In the daytime, if the storm cell is really active, try firing off frames as fast as your camera will allow. Be prepared to waste a lot of film this way; but if conditions are right, you should be able to intercept at least one strike on a roll (see pp. 104-105). You can increase the odds by using relatively slow film (ISO 50) or smaller lens apertures (f/16-f/32) to lengthen exposure times. There is a device to trigger a camera electronically when it senses the first lightning stroke; but in my experience, manual shooting delivers results that are as good or better.

Shooting at night is easier. You'll want a camera that will allow you to make time exposures—one with "B" or "T" settings for long exposures of five seconds or more. A cable release is also useful to lock the shutter open; otherwise you must hold the shutter release button down manually during the entire exposure. The lens opening (aperture) determines how much light will reach the film, and the preferred setting will depend upon the film speed (ISO) and your distance from the storm—begin with f/5.6 for ISO 100 film. Focus on the storm (it had better be at "infinity"!), open the shutter, wait for one or more lightning flashes, and then close the shutter when you have what you want. The hardest part is connecting with ideal shooting conditions, and that comes with experience in predicting storm behavior, many hours on the road, and a certain amount of good luck.

Chasing lightning can be fun, but it's also a risky business. Shoot from within a car or a building if the storm is nearby. Although standing on a hilltop during an electrical storm is exhilarating, it's far from safe. Remember, if you can hear thunder, you're close enough to be struck by lightning, even when no cloud is overhead.

WHITE SAND + BLACK LAVA are exposure challenges. Most cameras purported to have fully automatic everything still can't think. All light meters are calibrated to read neutral gray (18% light reflectance) as the average; anything that varies widely from that value cannot be properly understood by any camera's meter. Using the point-and-shoot approach, white sand will come out gray every time, and so will black lava.

To get properly exposed photographs, you must compensate for difficult lighting situations. Some cameras offer settings for different types of scenes—bright landscapes or heavy shade, for example—while others have an exposure compensation dial, usually numbered in increments from +3 to -3. The first type is easier to use but allows much less control over the result. If you have a dial, add exposure for scenes brighter than "average" (move in the "+" direction; for dark scenes, subtract exposure (move in the "-" direction).

Knowing how much to compensate requires judgment and experience, and to gain it I recommend shooting three or four pictures of each scene bracketed in increments of one-half in the direction you know will be necessary. Use slide film and keep notes. With print film, you'll have trouble when the negatives are machine-printed. Printing machines are set to print every image as an average exposure. So your white sand will come out gray again, even if you have a perfectly exposed negative. The only way around this is to have negatives custom-printed, and you'll need to explain to the lab that the sand should be white.

SUNSETS + SILHOUETTES are a trademark of the Southwest. But capturing their magic on film can be difficult, especially if you have a fully automatic camera. Pointing the camera directly into the setting sun will underexpose your photographs, much as when shooting white sand.

To expose a sunset properly, try composing the picture with the setting sun away from the center of the frame (the built-in light meter gathers most of its reading from the center) or wait until the sun has dropped below the horizon. You should also try your camera's exposure compensation feature(s) discussed above—use the "bright scene" setting or add about +1 to improve the exposure. If you have a camera with fully adjustable settings or own a hand-held light meter, take your reading from a neutral area of blue or gray or deep red in the mid-tone range between the brightest and darkest areas in the scene.

Another trick for success with fully automatic cameras is to include a tree or other object in front of the painted sky. A silhouette will add interest to the photograph and at the same time help to brighten the sunset. The camera's light meter takes part of its reading from the dark object in the foreground and part from the sky, a mix that often gives a well-balanced exposure.

E q u i p m e n t + F i l m are tools of the trade. The first question many people ask when they see a captivating photograph is "What kind of camera do you use?" This, I feel, is akin to asking a chef what kind of oven created that delectable dessert. In the hands of a professional, all leading cameras will perform superbly. The issue is creative performance, not brand.

   Camera format and film type are more important concerns. I shoot in 35mm, 6x7cm, and 6x17cm panoramic formats, equipment that offers the speed and versatility needed for diverse subject matter. And for many aesthetic and technical reasons, my favorite films are in the Fujichrome line.

E x p e r i m e n t — all professionals do on a regular basis. Film is the least expensive part of one's travels. Experimentation leads to growth and rewarding discoveries in photography, as in so many other fields. Above all, enjoy the experience, and remember Sir Francis Bacon's advice: "The best part of beauty is that which no picture can express."

T h o m a s W i e w a n d t
T u c s o n , A r i z o n a

P h o t o g r a p h s ,   p r e c e d i n g   p a g e s

Opening Page: Pursuing a jackrabbit in the Eureka Dunes, Death Valley National Park, California

Title Page: Storm clearing over Bryce Canyon National Park, Utah

Copyright Page: Balloon over Monument Valley, Utah

Epigraph + Dedication: Young barrel cactus in Joshua Tree National Park, California

Table of Contents: SP Crater in the San Francisco Volcanic Field, Arizona;
   North Rim of the Grand Canyon

Preface + Acknowledgments: Cliff Rose in Grand Canyon National Park, Arizona

Face

"People have been looking into this country for a long time, loving it, cursing it, gutting it, changing it, enduring it. Not all have found it to be beautiful. Many have come to know parts of it very well; few have come to know all of it." C. GREGORY CRAMPTON

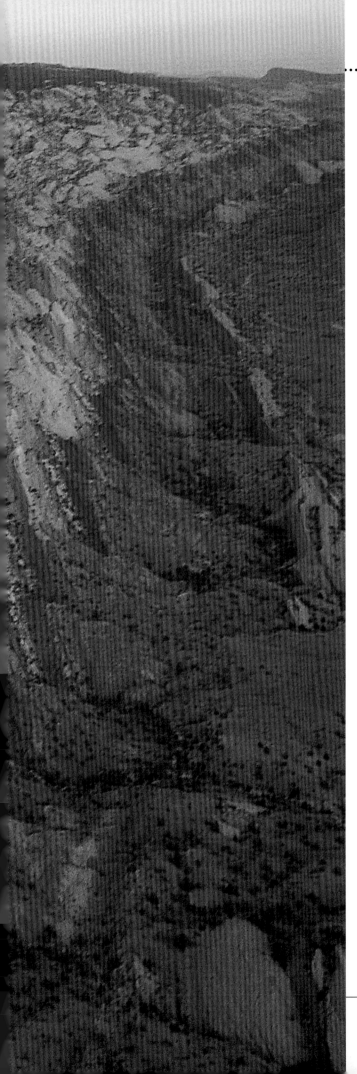

THE DISCOVERY OF GOLD in California in 1848 fueled a massive westward movement of fortune-seekers. The start of the journey from the Mississippi River did not appear too daunting—grass-covered plains spread as far as the eye could see. But weeks later, a rugged obstacle loomed on the horizon—the Rocky Mountains—the first of many challenging landscapes that would lie ahead.

While most emigrants chose the easier northern route around the Colorado Rockies, others skirted the southern end to Santa Fe. From this early Spanish settlement, pioneers followed an old trail northwest through red-rock country, a vast tableland dominated by cliffs, canyons, and monumental sandstone formations—a region known today as the **Colorado Plateau.**

Aerial view of the Waterpocket Fold, a gigantic, step-like wrinkle in the Earth's crust that forms the centerpiece of Capitol Reef National Park in Utah.

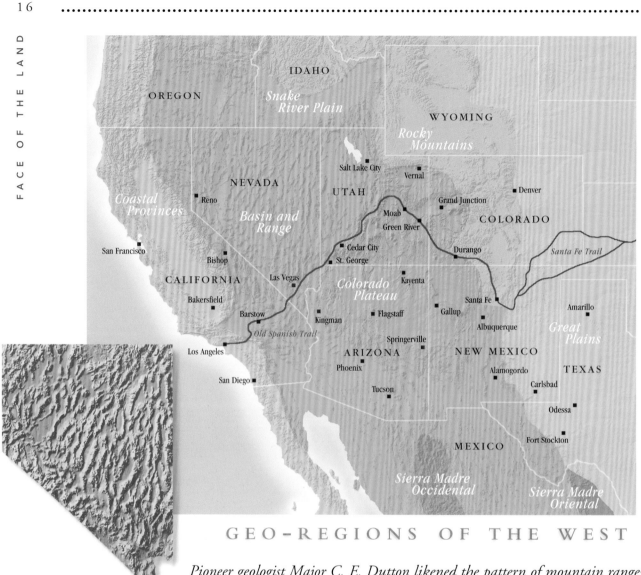

GEO-REGIONS OF THE WEST

Pioneer geologist Major C. E. Dutton likened the pattern of mountain ranges in Nevada to "an army of caterpillars crawling northward out of Mexico."

The trail then wound its tortuous way through an endless barrage of mountain ranges and desert valleys in southern Nevada and California, across what geologists call the **Basin and Range Province.** According to historian Leroy Hafen, this Old Spanish Trail was "the longest, crookedest, most arduous pack-mule route in the history of America."

Those who completed the journey ended up in the slow-paced town of Los Angeles, only recently claimed from Mexico. To get there, they had crossed five of the seven distinct geographical regions of the West (see map), each with a different geological history. Two of these regions dominate the Southwest: the Colorado Plateau and the Basin and Range.

Each of the above regions has a distinctive geological history. This book focuses on the Colorado Plateau and much of the Basin and Range.

The Colorado Plateau—named in honor of the river that carved its most dramatic canyons—is an elevated expanse of layered rock that formed long before the Age of Dinosaurs. At times during its genesis, the region lay submerged beneath shallow seas; at other times, it was dry and buried beneath shifting dunes. As mud, sand, and silt accumulated over millions of years, pressure from the weight of layers upon layers increased and mineral-rich water cemented the particles together, transforming these sediments to rock.

LIVING LANDSCAPES
The four desert regions of North America.
Each has a different climate

GREAT BASIN DESERT

MOJAVE DESERT

SONORAN DESERT

CHIHUAHUAN DESERT

DESERT REGIONS

Dominating the Southwest are four desert regions—Great Basin, Mojave, Chihuahuan, Sonoran— each distinct and different from the geological regions. These, you might say, are bio-scapes, the living landscapes that clothe this world of rock

All except the Sonoran Desert have cold winters; and the **Great Basin Desert** *is the coldest—snow is common. The Great Basin is a shrub desert with few trees or succulents; sagebrush predominates. Though often freezing in the winter, the* **Mojave Desert** *(also spelled* **Mohave***) can be scorching in the summer—it's home to Death Valley. The Joshua tree, a giant yucca, is one of the few tree-sized plants that grows here. The* **Chihuahuan Desert** *dominates the vast plateau of northcentral Mexico and the Mexican state of*

Chihuahua; despite winter cold, this region has a surprisingly rich assortment of shrubs, small cacti, yuccas, and century plants. Warmest of all is the **Sonoran Desert,** *named after the Mexican state of Sonora; north of the border, temperatures occasionally dip below freezing. This is a relatively lush desert dominated by leguminous trees and cactus giants, one of which, the saguaro, has become a scenic icon of the American Southwest.*

WHAT IS THE GREAT BASIN?

The **Great Basin** *is a large, generally dry, mountain-studded region of the West where no rivers flow to the sea. Streams disappear into the sand. Surface water collects in a few shallow, salty lakes within this vast drainage basin, which encompasses most of Nevada*

and smaller portions of five other states. Utah's Great Salt Lake, Nevada's Pyramid Lake, and California's Mono Lake are three of the biggest; the majority of the others are dry most of the time.

In contrast, geologists delineate the **Basin and Range** *region by its distinctive geological history rather than by its drainage pattern. Here, blocks of the Earth's crust have shifted along fault lines, creating a region of uplifted mountain ranges separated by down-dropped valley basins (also known as grabens). The Basin and Range (technically a physiographic province) extends much farther south, embracing southern Arizona and New Mexico, the western corner of Texas, and adjacent parts of Mexico (see map, page 16).*

About the time dinosaurs disappeared, profound changes in landscapes of the Southwest took place. Strange as this might sound, even solid rock—under slow, steady pressure—can bend and fold like taffy. Movements in the Earth's crust squeezed, crumpled, and sometimes cracked rocky layers of the embryonic Colorado Plateau and forced mountain ranges to rise around it. Much later, a mere 10 million years ago, pressure from below forced the plateau to rise as a unit, to elevations as high as 10,000 feet (3,050 m). As rivers and streams whittled way at the surface of this massive block of sediments, canyons took shape and folds in the layered rock were exposed, features that dominate the region today. Troublesome to get over or around, the more formidable ridges and escarpments were called **reefs** by early European settlers, harking back to their seafaring days.

LAYERS

Though cursed by early settlers, the intricately sculpted surface of the Colorado Plateau now draws tourists from around the world. Among its scenic attractions are dramatic wrinkles in the Earth's crust that now lie exposed by erosion (see preceding text), many of which are showcased in Utah. These colorful, tilted layers of rock appear as step-like folds, upfolds, downfolds, or narrow, steep-sided ridges, known to geologists as **monoclines, anticlines, synclines,** *or* **hogbacks,** *respectively.*

MONOCLINES
STEP-LIKE FOLDS

A spectacular step-like break in the Earth's crust that stretches for almost 100 miles down the backbone of Capitol Reef National Park— the Waterpocket Fold— is a monocline. Native Americans have called its colorful cliffs and twisting canyons the "Land of the Sleeping Rainbow"(see chapter opener.)

Other prominent monoclines include the Cockscomb in Grand Staircase-Escalante National Monument; Comb Ridge, which is crossed by two scenic highways in southeastern Utah, Route 95 west of Blanding and Route 163 west of Bluff; and the San Rafael Swell, crossed by Interstate 70 about 15 miles west of Green River, Utah.

HOGBACKS

These narrow, linear ridges of steeply tilted layers formed as erosion stripped away the softer underlying rock, leaving harder layers protruding high above the desert floor. Undulating hogback ridges surround the Visitors Center in Dinosaur National Monument, and a prominent hogback crosses Route 64 just west of Farmington, New Mexico.

ANTICLINES
UPFOLDS

Just north of Monument Valley and due east of Mexican Hat Rock—seen from scenic Route 163—is a striking slope of sandstone chevrons, the western flank of Raplee Anticline. Locals sometimes refer to this colorful patchwork of rock layers as the "Indian Blanket." Travel a little farther east, en route to Bluff, and you'll see another astounding anticline known as Lime Ridge—its beautiful eastern slope faces the Comb Ridge monocline.

Featured in the Island in the Sky district of Canyonlands National Park is a unique doughnut-like depression known as the Upheaval Dome. Its origin remains a mystery. Some geologists propose that it is a circular anticline, while others are convinced that it is a meteorite crater.

SYNCLINES
DOWNFOLDS

U-shaped folds that dip into level rock layers, called synclines, usually run parallel to those that bulge upward (anticlines). Prominent synclines cross Route 160 between Tuba City and Kayenta, Arizona. Rainbow Basin, located about eight miles north of Barstow, California, is an especially colorful syncline.

A HOGBACK, NOT OF THE BARNYARD KIND

Throughout the Southwest, especially on the Colorado Plateau, you might see prominent ridges of steeply tilted, layered rock, a hogback to geologists (below). This one in northwestern New Mexico is simply called "The Hogback." Harder layers—those covering the left-facing slope of the ridge—wear away more slowly than the underlying layers, exposed along the steeper slope to the right.

Several dramatic folds in layered rock of the Colorado Plateau are beautifully exposed in southeastern Utah. Among them is the up-warped Raplee Anticline (above), which drops to the San Juan River near Mexican Hat. Sandstone layers that have eroded into chevron patterns—flatirons—suggest those primitive appliances used by early pioneer women.

The Upheaval Dome (left), in Canyonlands National Park—where did it come from? No one can agree— some say it's from forces below; others think a rock from space did the work. Photo by William Dupré.

Illustrations by David Fischer with Leo Gabaldon as consultant

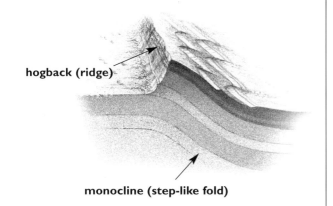

hogback (ridge)

monocline (step-like fold)

upfold (anticline)   **downfold (syncline)**

The Southwest's other major geographical region—the Basin and Range—lies west and south of the Colorado Plateau. Here, over the last 15 million years, the land stretched, thinned, and broke into blocks. In zones of tension and instability along cracks between these enormous blocks—known as **faults**—some blocks slid up and others down, creating a region with hundreds of mountain ranges alternating with long, linear valleys (see illustration). Nevada alone has 413 such ranges. At the lowest point in the Western Hemisphere, at Badwater in Death Valley, you can stand 282 feet (86 m) below sea level and gaze across the valley floor to faulted mountains that rise over 11,000 feet (3,350 m) above you.

Unlike the relatively stable Colorado Plateau, the Basin & Range region has remained prone to earthquakes. In 1872, history's largest quake in the American Southwest struck Owens Valley, California, stopping clocks and awakening people as far away as San Diego. It destroyed 52 of Lone Pine's 59 houses, and killed 27 people. One report claimed that the first shock waves threw fish onto the riverbank, so that "men stopping there who were engaged in building a boat did not hesitate to capture them, and served them up for breakfast in the morning—a quite novel method of utilizing an earthquake."

In December 1849, a weary band of about 100 pioneers—seeking a "shortcut" to the California goldfields—descended the Black Mountains to the barren, salt-encrusted floor of Death Valley. The towering Panamint Range blocked their westward progress. Over the next two months, as they searched for and found a desolate route out of the valley, the settlers used their wagons for fuel, ate their oxen, and abandoned most of their goods. Yet despite their legendary suffering, which gave the valley its name, only one member died.

ENDLESS MOUNTAINS

Mountain scenery of the type found in southern Arizona (left) is a typical Basin and Range landscape. Above, two impressive mountain ranges, the Black Mountains in the foreground and the snow-capped Panamints behind, flank the eastern and western sides of the Death Valley basin, respectively. The diagram to the right illustrates the origin of Basin and Range topography, a process called block faulting.

formation of mountain ranges and valley basins

Gold to Ghost Towns

DURING the past 150 years, the pursuit of precious metals—gold, silver, and copper—has shaped lore and landscapes of the American Southwest. The first wave of prospectors came to mine gold from stream gravels in California's Sierra Nevada. When the easy surface gold was taken, diggers searched for—and found—the source of the gold.

Miners dug tunnels to follow veins underground. With each new discovery, or strike, crude towns blossomed overnight. When riches dwindled, boomtowns went bust.

Silver—usually found with deposits of zinc or lead—ushered in the second wave of prospecting and settlement. Virginia City, Nevada; Bodie, California; Tombstone, Arizona; and Leadville, Colorado, are names linked with silver mining in the West. Tombstone, founded in 1877 and known as "The Town Too Tough to Die," grew up around mining claims. By 1881, its population had climbed to 6,000, complete with gamblers and gunmen. Reflecting Tombstone's legendary violence, Boothill Cemetery holds the remains of more than 250 people, only a handful of whom died of natural causes. Although the boomtown days were brief—less than 10 years—Tombstone has survived into the 21st century as a center of ranching, movie-making, and tourism.

"Forgive me, God—I'm going to Bodie," a child is reported to have prayed as she accompanied her parents to California. Bodie's silver mines supported a thriving community of more than 10,000 in the 1870s, yielding almost $100 million in ore. But when the silver veins played out, the town died. Today, Bodie is one of the best preserved ghost towns in the West—more than 100 original buildings have survived fire and neglect. It's also a beautiful, isolated, and evocative place to visit. Lupine and sagebrush now surround the rustic wooden buildings in Bodie State Historic Park.

DUSTY MEMORIES

The historical remains of Bodie (above & lower right)—one of many 19th century silver-mining boomtowns gone bust.

THE LIVING DEAD

Unlike Bodie, Tombstone hasn't died altogether.
Surviving as a small semi-ghost town, tourists come
from around the world to visit the place "where the
legend lives on." One favorite stop is Boothill
Cemetery (right).

Copper Mining, Then + Now

COPPER MINING followed silver, as silver had followed gold. Early underground mines like those at Bisbee, Clifton, and Morenci, Arizona, were replaced in 1937 by huge open-pit operations. Phelps Dodge's Morenci mine, in eastern Arizona, remains the second largest copper producer in North America and the sixth largest in the world. In 1996, the mine yielded over 1 billion pounds of copper—23.6% of the U.S. output and 5.1% of the world production.

Since World War II, demand for copper has dropped, and, over the years, Arizona's less profitable mining operations have been shut down, tied in part to tighter controls over air and water pollution. When mines closed in the thriving communities of Jerome and Bisbee in 1953 and 1975, respectively, they quickly became ghost towns. Jerome's population fell from 15,000 in the Roaring Twenties to less than 100 in the late 1950s. Bisbee's fate was similar; but both have slowly made comebacks as artist, retirement, and tourist towns. Thirteen copper mines remain active in Arizona, still our nation's primary source of this useful metal.

In southern Arizona, underground copper mining began in the 1870s but gave way to huge open-pit operations in the 1930s. Miners from the Morenci District posed for the photograph below around 1900. Today, the mine (left) is populated by monster machines (right) and relatively small crews. Unlike the chunk of raw, native copper featured on the opposite page, most ore contains little copper; and to cost-effectively extract the mineral, it must be dissolved and concentrated in solution.

MONSTER MACHINE

To hold title as North America's second biggest producer of copper, Arizona's Morenci mining operation runs 24 hours per day, seven days per week. The force of nearly 100 enormous 240- to 360-ton haul trucks burns up to 100 gallons of diesel fuel per truck per hour. Each 320-ton truck carries a price tag of $2.2 million; and each tire—with a life expectancy of six months—costs $24,000. The 15 giant electric shovels used to fill these trucks are even more pricey, $8 million each.

Photo courtesy of the Phelps Dodge Corporation

Copper Country

ROCKS are made up of **minerals**—there are over 4,000 of them known to science. And minerals are made up of **elements**—calcium, copper, iron, and oxygen, for example. Ninety elements occur in nature, and another 20 are human creations. Everything around us, and in us—from silicon chips and neon lights to DNA and the food we eat—is made from these basic elements, and seventy-five percent of them are metals. These include gold, copper, silver, and iron.

Copper has been treasured for thousands of years in the Southwest—first by Native Americans who used coppery minerals to adorn pottery, and later by industrialists, who manufactured pipes and wire. This metal has long been so important to the economy of Arizona that the state flag bears a copper-colored star and copper forms the dome of the state capitol building.

Copper is tightly woven into the fabric of our lives. The skin of the Statue of Liberty is made of copper right down to the rivets and joints. The Mineral Information Institute estimates that every American born will use 1,925 pounds of copper in a lifetime, mostly in the form of electrical wire, pipes for plumbing, utility cable, automotive

parts, doorknobs, keys, and coins. The U.S. "golden" Sacajawea dollar is made from an alloy of copper, zinc, manganese, and nickel. And a new generation of computer processors is being made with copper because this metal is an excellent conductor, second only to silver.

Besides its native, or raw, mineral form, copper comes in other guises: among them are turquoise, malachite, and azurite. Of these three copper-bearing gemstones, turquoise is the most valuable. Among southwestern tribes, turquoise is sacred and the color associated with the cardinal direction south. To the Navajo, it's a part of the sky fallen to Earth. The Zuni and Apache wore pieces of turquoise as jewelry or carried them as amulets in leather medicine pouches for protection from demons and to aid hunters.

COPPER SAVES THE LADY

Our great symbol of freedom and international good will, the Statue of Liberty, has survived beautifully since its dedication in 1886, primarily because she wears a copper shield against the elements. Photo by Joseph Sohm

COPPER IN COINS

The U. S. Golden Dollar is a copper sandwich that's 88.5% copper; the "golden" faces of this coin are a special alloy of 77% copper, 12% zinc, 7% manganese, and 4% nickel

New U. S. Quarters, Dimes, and Half Dollars are also copper sandwiches, each 91.7% copper.

Even the U.S. Nickel is 75% copper; but today's copper colored U.S. Penny is only 2.6% copper—its core is mostly zinc, with a thin coating of copper

COPPER IN DISGUISE

A multitude of minerals are laden with copper, including a few treasured gemstones: turquoise (above, in a vein), malachite (opposite right, cut), and azurite (opposite left—vibrant blue nodules on an uncut surface of malachite).

POPPIES ON COPPER

The Mexican gold poppy (opposite bottom), a spring wildflower that puts on a traffic-stopping show in the Sonoran Desert in favorable years, is also fond of copper—it thrives in copper-rich soils.

Recycled Scenery

THE DISTINCTIVE ROCKY LANDSCAPES of the Southwest—from the colorful mesas and buttes of the Colorado Plateau to the dry desert floor of Death Valley—nearly all began in liquid form deep within the Earth. Their journey from molten rock to the scenic icons of Monument Valley involved many miraculous transformations along the way.

All rocks and minerals follow a cycle of breakdown and rebirth, a process driven by earth movements. The thin **crust** that shields us from the fire within our planet resembles a giant, dynamic jigsaw puzzle. It is broken into eight huge slabs and more than a dozen smaller ones carried atop a plastic, partially molten layer below. These rigid slabs, **tectonic plates,** are kept in motion by molten rock as it slowly circulates between hotter and cooler places within the Earth, similar to the way soup circulates in a pot heated on the stove.

Magma—a fiery soup of liquid rock and suspended solids such as crystals and rock fragments—crystallizes to form **igneous** (Latin for *fire-formed*) **rocks.** When magma rises to the surface during volcanic eruptions and emerges as lava, it cools quickly into small-crystal rocks such as *basalt, andesite,* or *rhyolite.* Alternatively, this magma soup may solidify underground to form large-crystal igneous rocks such as *granite.* Shifting tectonic plates thrust these underground masses to the surface, creating many of the Southwest's high mountain ranges—the Sandias just east of Albuquerque, the Santa Catalinas by Tucson, and the Black Mountains on the east side of Death Valley, for example.

CALIFORNIA RUMBLIN'

California is part of the Pacific "Ring of Fire," a zone of violent geological unrest that surrounds the Pacific Ocean Basin. Much of the Pacific sea floor is actually an enormous piece of the Earth's crust, a tectonic plate. The Ring falls along the edges of this plate and is an active earthquake zone that contains over 75% of the world's volcanoes. And the San Andreas Fault—only one of many in California—is among the longest and most active in the world. Other spots around the Pacific plate, notably Japan and Alaska, have more earthquakes, but California ranks high on the list with an average of 500 shocks felt by residents each year.

Visitors to western mountains and plateaus are often greeted by the golden-mantled ground squirrel (left), seen here atop a granite boulder in the Sierra Nevada range.

URANIUM

The nuclear arms race that followed World War II led to a demand for uranium. The Four Corners area became a leader in uranium production after a 1952 discovery of the element in sandstones southeast of Moab, Utah. Worldwide, uranium ore is widespread. Today the largest high-grade uranium mines are in Saskatchewan, Canada, but Australia has the largest deposits. Uranium is now in greatest demand for use as fuel in nuclear power plants; nuclear power currently supplies approximately 17% of the world's electricity. Only 20% of the electricity generated in the United States comes from nuclear power, compared to 77% in France.

Radioactive decay from uranium, thorium, and potassium deep within the Earth releases energy in the form of heat that slowly rises to the surface, contributing to the gradual drift of continental land masses over the face of our planet.

BORN IN FIRE

Lava (opposite, top) and all granites arose from the fiery underworld. Because granitic rocks are haphazardly organized clusters of crystals, they weather into rounded shapes, as seen in the monzogranite boulders in Joshua Tree National Park (opposite, bottom). A canyon treefrog spends its day concealed on a granitic outcrop (with large quartz crystals) in Tucson's Santa Catalina Mountains (opposite, center).

The element uranium (right) has been found in small amounts worldwide within fire-formed rocks or ancient layers of sediment on the Colorado Plateau.

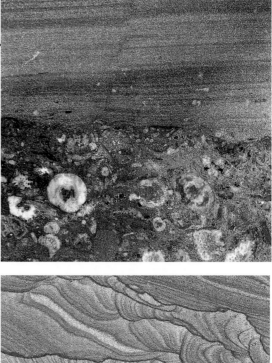

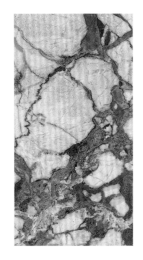

Rocks exposed at the surface are slowly broken down into smaller particles by erosion. Boulders are reduced to cobbles, gravel, sand, and eventually to fine silty mud and clay. As these deposits accumulate over time, layer upon layer, along with plant and animal remains, the deeper layers are compressed and cemented into common **sedimentary rocks,** such as *sandstone, mudstone,* and *shale.* And in ancient sea beds, particles of shell and coral fuse to form *limestone.* Much of the flat and fancifully carved geo-scenery on the Colorado Plateau, including Monument Valley, is made of sedimentary rock.

The ground we stand on is in motion, just as it has been for millions of years. Geologically speaking, tectonic plates are still moving fast today, about as fast as human fingernails grow; and given enough time, astonishing things can happen. When plates collide, rocky surface layers of the plates may fold downwards, or one plate might even plunge deep beneath another. Squeezed and baked in a changed chemical environment, the rocks experience a metamorphosis. Their grains recrystallize into new minerals, and **metamorphic** (Latin for *changed form*) **rocks**— such as *gneiss* (pronounced "nice"), a coarsely crystalline, banded rock, and *schist,* a mica-rich rock—are born. Both occur in the dark-colored walls of Colorado's famous Black Canyon of the Gunnison and on canyon floors in Colorado National Monument. Beds of water-worn schist can be seen at the very bottom of the Grand Canyon.

When rocks are buried even deeper, they melt and begin the cycle over again.

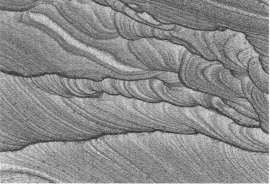

ROCKS REBORN

On the restless surface of our planet, some rocks get sent back to the womb, so to speak, deep underground. And if conditions are right, they will partially melt and recrystallize into a new type of rock—metamorphic rock. Marble (top left and near right) and gneiss (in circle) are common rocks that were transformed in this way.

LAYER UPON LAYER

The intricately eroded amphitheater of Bryce Canyon National Park (right) began as stacked-up layers of silt, sand, and limy sediments from the shells and skeletons of living animals. A slice through a block of limestone (near left, top)—one type of sedimentary rock—shows fragments of fossilized sea "lilies" (crinoids). Another type, sandstone (near left, middle), dominates the Colorado Plateau.

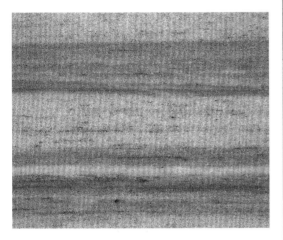

The highest cliff in Colorado, the Black Canyon of the Gunnison's Painted Wall, rises 2,240 feet (683 m) above the Gunnison River (below). Its walls of metamorphic rock fractured under stress eons ago. The cracks filled with a fiery mineral soup that cooled and hardened into the veins of igneous rock that "paint" the wall today.

OVERLEAF ▶

Layered, taffy-like swirls of sandstone in the Paria Canyon-Vermilion Cliffs Wilderness along the Arizona-Utah border.

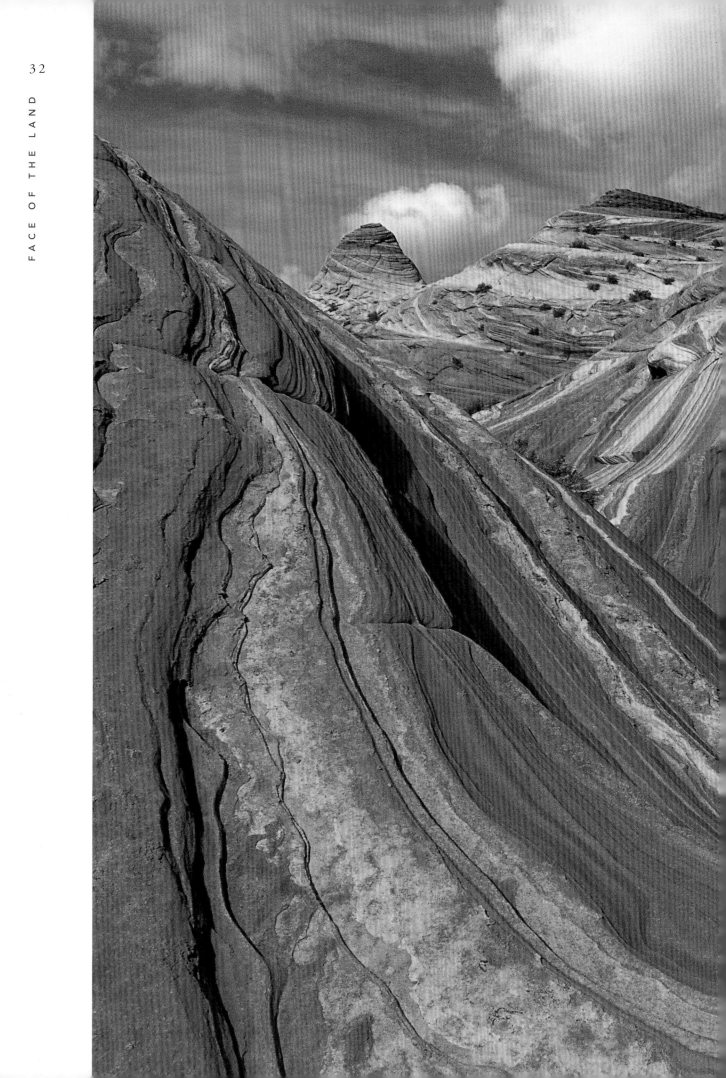

Crystals + Gemstones

MOST MINERALS that grow in liquids solidify with geometric precision, forming **crystals** (a three-dimensional latticework of atoms that grows as more atoms attach themselves, layer upon layer, to exposed surfaces). Deep within the Earth, crystals often develop in red-hot fluids—quartz, mica, corundum (ruby and sapphire), and the perfect prisms of emerald and aquamarine, for example. Others, such as salt and gypsum, crystallize in evaporating desert lakes. With few exceptions, **rocks** are imperfect masses of millions of tightly interlocking crystals, often too tiny to be evident.

Gemstones can be single crystals or a mix of minerals—including rocks—shaped and polished to reveal their exquisite beauty. **Quartz** is one of the two most abundant rock-forming minerals in the Earth's crust; **feldspar** is the other. There are more than 35 varieties of quartz alone, many of which are considered gemstones, including *amethyst, citrine, agate, jasper,* and *tiger's-eye.* The crystals in agate and jasper are microscopic. *Turquoise* and *malachite* are among those gemstones that display a solid, earthy texture, less elegant than the translucent stones perhaps, but stunningly colorful nonetheless.

CRYSTALS BEGET ROCKS

Although often invisible to the naked eye, nearly all rocks are imperfect masses of crystals. The two most abundant rock-forming minerals are feldspar and quartz (the feldspar specimen above contains a large crystal of smoky quartz). Tiger's-eye, rose quartz, amethyst, citrine, and agate (below) are among the many gemstone varieties of quartz. A gemstone that turns up in copper mines is turquoise (opposite, lower right). Another—a rare relative of lead—is wulfenite (right); the Southwest is among the few places in the world where it's found. Sugar also crystallizes in attractive shapes (bottom right).

ROCK CANDY

You can watch large sugar crystals (rock candy) grow in a super-saturated sugar solution. Simply dissolve 5 cups of sugar in 2 cups of water while heating. Then bring the syrup to a temperature of about 250°F (120°C), without stirring. Pour into a pyrex bottle or pan and sink a weighted string or wooden skewer stick into the solution; and allow it to cool undisturbed. Cover and wait for about a week. The crystals will grow on the string or stick. Rinse crystals quickly in cold water and let them dry.

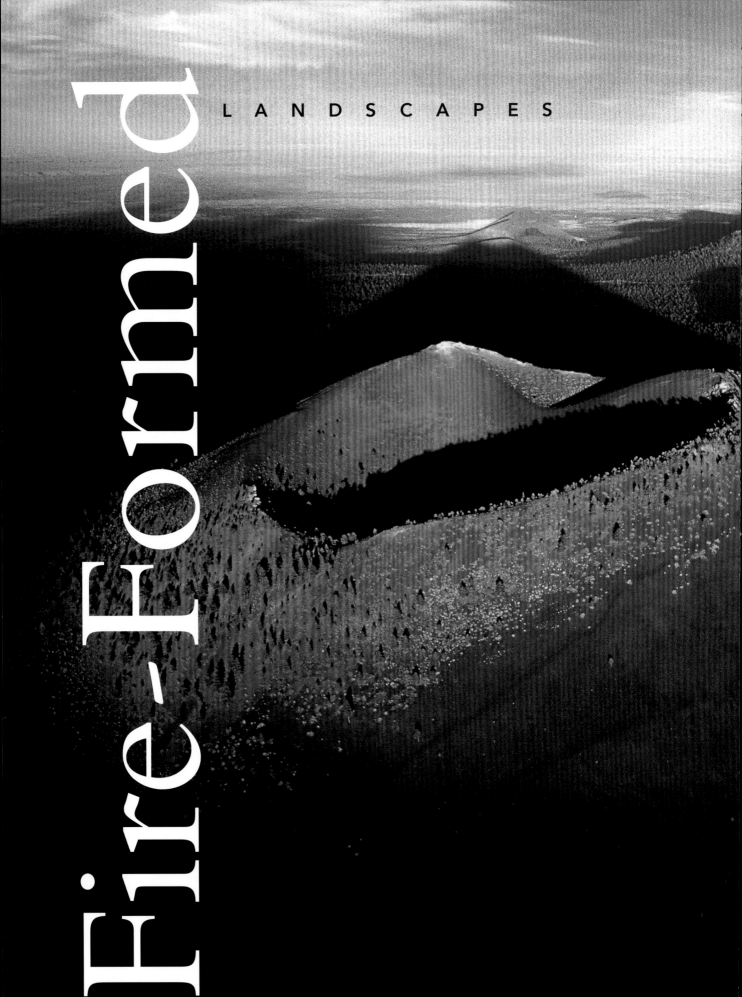

Fire-Formed

LANDSCAPES

"It is a . . . nightmarishly beautiful scene . . . which looks so newly wrecked that one almost expects to see the lava still smoking."

JOSEPH WOOD KRUTCH

TWO GREAT MOUNTAINS sacred to no less than five American Indian cultures lie in northern Arizona and New Mexico. It's said by the Navajo that to embellish their flat, sun-baked world, First Man and First Woman decided to change the landscape. To the west they added snow-topped *Dook'o'oosłííd,* San Francisco Mountain, and decorated it with animals and with the black clouds that produce harsh male rain. To the south they formed *Tsoodzil,* Mount Taylor, adorned it with turquoise and blue birds, and covered it with heavy mist that brings gentle, female rain. Today we know that both mountains are the remains of extinct volcanoes.

Sunset Crater Volcano National Monument, just north of Flagstaff, Arizona, showcases this impressive cinder cone.

Hundreds of cinder cones populate Arizona's San Francisco volcanic field, one of six hotspots in the Southwest that could roar back to life, given enough time. Among the youngest and most perfectly shaped is SP Crater, 26 miles north of Flagstaff—best seen from the air (above).

Indeed, volcanoes have formed and reformed many scenic landscapes of the American Southwest. In the past 35 million years alone, volcanoes have built solitary mountains like Mount Taylor and San Francisco Mountain, as well as Picacho Peak, the distinctive landmark that looms 1,500 feet above Interstate 10 between Phoenix and Tucson. Volcanoes have also created entire mountain ranges, including the San Juans in southwestern Colorado, New Mexico's Gila Mountains, the Superstitions and Chiricahuas in Arizona, and the Sierra del Pinacate of northwestern Mexico.

ANOTHER MOUNT ST. HELENS?

San Francisco Mountain (below)—a haven for skiers just north of Flagstaff—is actually a giant volcano. Geologists believe that its summit once towered 16,000-feet (4,900-m) before blowing its top some 300,000 years ago. Similarities to the fate of Mount St. Helens in 1980 (right) are striking. Today, six prominent San Francisco Peaks—the tallest being 12,633 feet (3,850 m)—surround its Inner Basin, the volcano's crater. Photo of Mount St. Helens by Michael Doukas /Cascades Volcano Observatory /USGS.

VOLCANIC FEATURES OF THE SOUTHWEST

VN = VOLCANIC NECK (A monolith of volcanic rock jutting up from the surrounding landscape. This plug of hard lava once sat in the throat of a volcano—see page 52.)

VF = VOLCANIC FIELD (clusters of many small volcanoes, which may include cinder cones, craters, fissures, lava flows and domes) active within the past 5 million years

NP = NATIONAL PARK

NM = NATIONAL MONUMENT

SP = STATE PARK

NRA = NATIONAL RECREATION AREA

Volcanoes Not Expected to Re-awaken

Potentially Hazardous Volcanic Centers

Rio Grande Rift Valley

The mid-section of our continent is literally being torn apart by forces deep within the Earth, an event that began about 30 million years ago and continues today. It's happening along a valley bounded by fractures in the Earth's crust—the Rio Grande Rift. Within this zone, molten rock (lava) periodically rises and spreads across the surface. And in the not-too-distant future, geologically speaking—several million years or so—New Mexico may be divided by an inland seaway.

MOST DANGEROUS VOLCANO

Within a 48-hour period in November 1997, more than a thousand earthquakes shook southern California's Long Valley. Earthquake swarms have been a daily occurrence there for the past 20 years, though most are small tremors that go unnoticed by residents. A magma-fed bulge within this ancient 10-by-20-mile crater has risen 31 inches (79 cm) since 1979; and, since 1994, carbon dioxide leaking from cracks in the mountain has killed acres of trees. The cataclysmic,

explosive eruption that created this volcanic field about 760,000 years ago is believed to have been a thousand times greater than that of Mount St. Helens. Residents and visitors alike should be aware that Long Valley—with California's largest ski area—has high potential for another volcanic eruption. Scientists with the USGS Volcano Hazards Program feel certain it will blow but can't predict when. They remain nervous and monitor geologic unrest in the area daily.

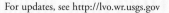

For updates, see http://lvo.wr.usgs.gov

Travelers are most surprised by the really young volcanic features, those that seem on a hot summer's day to be fresh and still cooling. Vast expanses of barren, unworn lava thousands of years old remind us that plant colonization and recovery are extremely slow in arid lands. No less than ten parks in the Greater Southwest showcase awesome landscapes of volcanic craters, cones, and lava flows.

Although the Southwest hasn't experienced a volcanic eruption for 250 years (the last one created Pahoa Island in Mono Lake, California), in many places, magma-heated waters bubble at the surface as hot springs.

Sites with such **geothermal** (Greek for *earth heat*) activity offer tremendous potential for generating electrical power. Steam, heat, and hot water from underground reservoirs provide the force that spins the turbine generators to produce electricity. A few geothermal power plants are now operating in California, Nevada, Utah, and Mexico with great success.

Compared to burning fossil fuels, this is a more efficient, more reliable, and cleaner source of energy. Northern California's Geysers Geothermal Facility, the world's largest, now supplies most of San Francisco's electricity. Its present capacity is 1,100 megawatts, enough power for a city of over a million people.

Geysers, bubbling mudpots, hot springs, and sulfur vents (below) are sure signs of a suitable place for generating electric power from Earth's internal heat. Holes drilled in such areas (left) allow engineers to extract energy in the form of steam, heat, or hot water.

Lava Flows to Cow-Pie Bombs

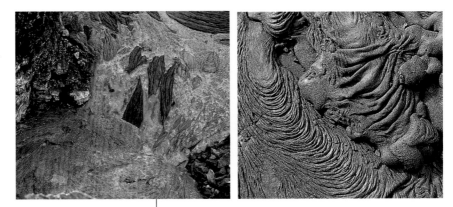

STARK PATCHES of black punctuate the colorful mesas, canyons, and mountains of the desert Southwest. These surreal, lunar landscapes—so extensive they can be seen from space—tell of a time when the region was alive with violent and spectacular volcanic eruptions. Here, the most fluid and common type of lava, basalt, spilled from the throats and sides of volcanoes and flowed across the desert floor.

Pahoehoe lava (*pah-hoy-hoy,* the Hawaiian word for *rope-like*) flows like molasses and looks ropy and rippled when it cools. Other basalt flows break up as they cool, leaving a jumble of jagged, upended blocks called clinkers. Layers of this **áá lava** (*ah-ah,* Hawaiian for *rough surface*) have glass-sharp edges that can shred a pair of hiking boots in less than a day. No wonder the Spanish called áá flows **malpais** (*MAL-pie-eese*), meaning *bad country.* Ropy and áá lavas are both prevalent in most of the younger volcanic fields of the Southwest (see map, pages 40-41). New Mexico's 44-mile-long Carrizozo lava flow is one of the world's longest (see Valley of Fires in Where to Find Them).

MOLTEN ROCK ON THE MOVE

How lava spreads across the land depends on its temperature and the minerals in it. The runniest is pahoehoe lava (above: hot, left; cool and solidified, right). Pahoehoe lava thickens as it cools and can begin to pile up and break into rough chunks, becoming áá lava. Photo of hot lava courtesy of the USGS.

A brittlebush has gained a foothold in an expanse of áá lava within Mexico's Pinacate Volcanic Field (left). And picturesque reminders of a lava flow over sandstone decorate Utah's Snow Canyon State Park (opposite, top)

MOST COMMON ROCK

Basalt covers more than 70% of the Earth's surface, much of it under the ocean. Most lava flows that blacken patches of the desert Southwest are basalt. Even on the moon, basalt is common— ancient basalt flows show up as the dark shadows we see on the face of the moon.

HOW HOT / HOW FAST?

The hottest lavas erupting from Kilauea, Hawaii, are close to 2,200°F (about 1,200°C). Compared in degrees Centigrade, lava would be 12 times hotter than boiling water, more than three times hotter than molten lead, but still below the melting temperature of iron (1,535°C).

Outrunning a lava flow doesn't take great athletic ability. Most people can easily walk two to four miles per hour; and at the front of a flow, the fastest lava on record in Hawaii advanced at about 6 miles/hour (10 km/hr). Lava flowing within an established channel is much, much faster, moving at speeds close to 37 mi/hr (60 km/hr).

Relatively tame volcanic eruptions like those typical of the Hawaiian Islands (left) produce rivers of lava—basalt—the most common rock on Earth. Photo by John Griggs/USGS

Basalt lavas, whether smooth-surfaced or jagged, come from **effusive volcanic eruptions.** Although such eruptions may begin as awesome, sometimes terrifying displays with fiery fountains or curtains of lava spouting from a volcano, they soon settle down and pour predictable streams of lava over the land. Although these flows incinerate buildings and plants along the way, people and animals can move fast enough to escape.

Not all lava is basalt. Thick, sluggish varieties of lava—some as thick as toothpaste—form when magma is enriched with silicon and oxygen on its way to the surface. Two common rock types that result are **rhyolite** (highest in silica) and **andesite** (intermediate between rhyolite and basalt). These rocks are lighter in color than basalt and come in shades of pink, purple, gray, pale brown, or white. In the Southwest, you can find rhyolite and andesite in both old and new volcanic landscapes, many of which are complex; geologists often need a magnifying lens to identify these rocks. Ask park personnel where to see them and keep your eyes open for clues. For example, the common rock around the ghost town of Rhyolite next to Death Valley is—you guessed it—rhyolite. Gila Cliff Dwellings in southwestern New Mexico is nestled in mountains of volcanic origin, and rangers will point out the andesite in a rocky layer below the cliff houses.

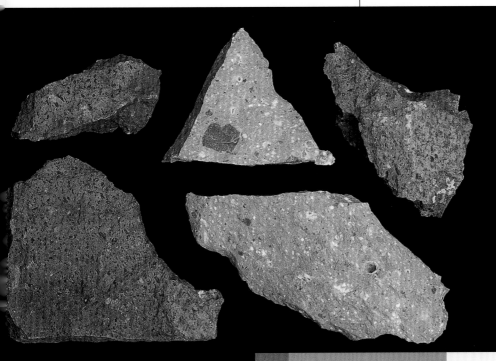

Rhyolite (left, the two lighter-colored pieces) and andesite (left, the three darker pieces) are rocks formed from thick, slow lava, while explosive eruptions may shower the ground with pellets of volcanic glass—"Apache Tears" (top center).

USEFUL VOLCANIC GLASS

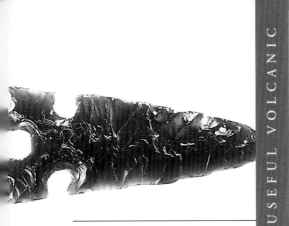

Obsidian is a dense volcanic glass, typically black in color, that formed when lava cooled too quickly for crystals to grow. Where violent, explosive eruptions took place, droplets of obsidian, called Apache Tears, litter the ground—you will probably see them for sale in southwestern gift shops.

Early Americans shaped obsidian into arrowheads and blades for hunting mammoths, bison, and deer.

When chipped, it fractures into smooth curves and holds a razor-sharp, serrated edge that can scratch steel. Today, because of its shine, jewelers value obsidian as a semi-precious stone.

Pumice rock floats on water because it is a solidified froth of volcanic glass and air bubbles. Pumice is used to stone-wash denim, make building blocks, remove calluses, and clean toilet bowls.

In contrast to effusive eruptions, **explosive eruptions**—like the one that sent ash clouds billowing thousands of feet into the air over Mount St. Helens in 1980—are not quiet outpourings of lava. Instead, they eject an ominous cloud of volcanic debris. Inside the volcano, gases build up, like those inside a shaken bottle of champagne; and when the inevitable explosion happens, molten rock blasts sky-high, often sending a glowing avalanche of ash, poisonous gases, and rock down the mountain at speeds up to 200 miles per hour (322 km/hr). Such **pyroclastic flows** flatten or burn everything in their path.

Geologists classify pyroclastic (Greek for *fire-fragments*) material by size. The finest particles, volcanic **dust** and **ash**, are so light that they can hang in the air as billowing clouds and travel for hundreds or thousands of miles. **Cinders** or lapilli (Italian for *little stones*) range from the size of a pea to that of a walnut. **Volcanic bombs**—molten fragments of basalt up to several feet in length—take on streamlined shapes because the lava is still soft as it flies through the air. Pieces that splat when they hit the ground are called **cow-pie bombs.** And bigger yet, sometimes as large as a house, are **blocks,** masses of solid rock torn apart by volcanic explosions.

When ash and other pyroclastic particles weld together in the presence of heat or moisture, they form **tuff,** a type of rock that's abundant near ancient explosive volcanoes. Both the Wonderland of Rocks in Arizona's Chiricahua National Monument and the City of Rocks State Park in southern New Mexico feature enormous boulders of eroded tuff. The canyon walls in Bandelier National Monument are also tuff, a soft variety that cliff-dwellers could chisel away to make room-sized alcoves.

Below: Hostile and stark landscape of Mexico's Pinacate Volcanic Field—a garden of desert delights.

Craters + Cones

IN A.D. 1064, EARTH-QUAKES rumbled on the east side of San Francisco Mountain in northern Arizona. Then, one morning, the ground split apart. Native Americans fled the area as fiery rocks shot into the air and sluggish streams of lava crept over the land. Sunset Crater Volcano gradually took shape. It may have taken less than ten years to form the colorful thousand-foot-tall (305-m) cinder cone we see today. And when the eruption ended, the people returned to rebuild their homes on top of the cinders. They had discovered that cinders hold moisture well, providing an excellent mulch for growing corn.

Throughout the Southwest, you can explore extinct volcanoes of all shapes and sizes. Each form depends upon the materials from which it

was built (see sidebar). Sunset Crater Volcano is a cinder cone with a shallow, funnel-shaped depression—a **crater**—at the top. The crater is all that remains of the vent through which rock, ash, and lava escaped when the volcano was alive.

Among the most unusual and spectacular craters on our continent are the **maar** (German for *lake*) **craters** of the Sierra del Pinacate in northwestern Mexico. The circular, cliff-lined maars took shape when molten rock mixed with water and triggered a sequence of steam explosions. No longer pots of roiling water, these awesome craters now collect sand from the Gran Desierto and shelter wild gardens of desert plants. More than a dozen maar volcanoes also occur in the northern part of Death Valley National Park, the largest of which is Ubehebe Crater. Panamint Indians called this place Ubehebe, *big basket in the rock.*

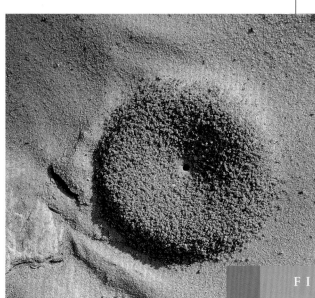

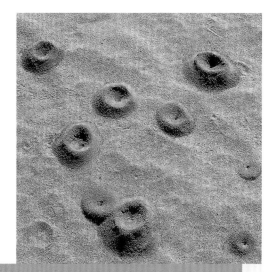

CRATERS, LARGE AND SMALL

Sand from Mexico's Gran Desierto dune field encroaches on MacDougal maar crater (left), the second largest in the Pinacate Volcanic Field. It is 400 feet (122 m) deep and was active about 185,000 years ago. Cratered landscapes in miniature (above) are pocked with cones built of sand instead of cinders.

Photo of MacDougal maar crater by Daniel J. Lynch; inset photo of the eruption of Paricutin in Mexico, facing page, by K. Segerstrom/USGS.

Another type of crater, a **caldera** (Spanish for *cauldron*) forms after a volcano has released huge volumes of molten rock and the ground above collapses into the empty space left by the escaping magma. Calderas range from a few miles across to giants that are clearly visible from space. California's Long Valley Caldera stretches for 20 miles (32 km), and New Mexico's Valles Caldera is 15 miles (24 km) rim-to-rim.

VOLCANOES — FIVE KINDS

CINDER CONE
A GIANT ANTHILL
Shaped like giant anthills, cinder volcanoes are steep-sided cones formed by layers of cinders and fine ash. There are hundreds of cinder cones in Mexico's Pinacate volcanic field and in northern Arizona's San Francisco volcanic field, Sunset Crater Volcano being the most famous. Capulin Volcano and Bandera Crater, both in New Mexico, are also cinder cones.

COMPOSITE CONE
A LAYER CAKE
Composite cones, also known as **strato-volcanoes,** are steep-sided and made from alternating layers of lava and ash. Layers are added with each eruption, a building process that often lasts tens to hundreds of thousands of years. Of the Earth's 1,511 volcanoes known to have erupted in the past 10,000 years, nearly half are composite volcanoes, including Mt. Taylor, San Francisco Mountain, Mount St. Helens, and many of the world's tallest volcanoes—Mt. Kilimanjaro and Mt. Fuji, for example.

SHIELD VOLCANO
THE LOW PROFILE
Bearing a name that's Icelandic in origin, shield volcanoes resemble a Viking warrior's shield lying face-up on the ground. They are produced by multiple eruptions of runny, basaltic lava that pile up, thin layer upon thin layer, over thousands of years, building gentle domes that cover a broad area. San Antonio Mountain in northern New Mexico and Volcan Santa Clara in Mexico's Sierra del Pinacate are shield volcanoes, as are the islands of Hawaii and their submarine foundations.

VOLCANIC DOME
A STEEP-SIDED LAVA MOUND
When thick, sticky, toothpaste-like lavas emerge from a volcano—too thick to flow—they build steep-sided cones, such as California's Lassen Peak. In the Southwest, a great concentration of volcanic domes lies immediately south of Mono Lake, California, forming the Mono-Inyo chain of more than a dozen rhyolite domes, part of the Long Valley volcanic center. Most of these small domes developed less than 10,000 years ago, and many are only 600 years old.

LAVA FLOODS
A LAVA PLAIN
Where the Earth's crust has pulled apart, thin, basaltic lavas that escape from the fissure can flood large areas to form tablelands like the Taos Plateau beneath the Rio Grande Valley. Some of the largest flood basalts occurred 65 million years ago in northwestern India, covering an area the size of Utah and Arizona combined—toxic gases released from these erupting fissures may have contributed to the extinction of dinosaurs.

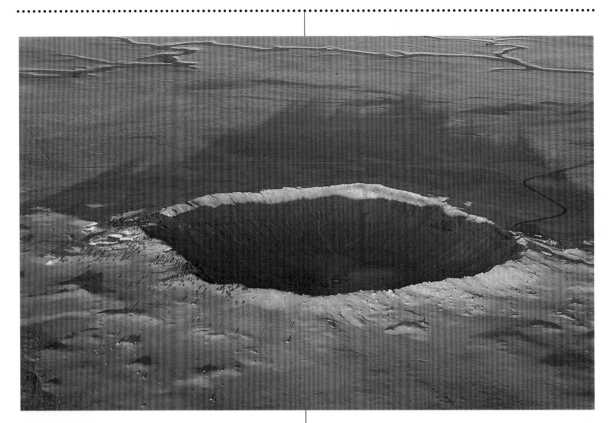

 Not all craters are volcanic in origin. When large chunks of extraterrestrial rock slam into the earth, **meteorite craters** are born, and Arizona is fortunate to have one of the world's best, a great scientific treasure for sure. Rocks from space that reach the ground are called **meteorites**; particles that burn up in the atmosphere as they fall are **meteors**. Meteors brighten the night sky for a brief moment as "falling stars," and most are tiny, about the size of a grain of sand. To Chumash tribes of southern California, a meteor was a person's soul on its way to the after-life. Although reports of people being killed by meteorites are extremely rare, collisions with Earth can have catastrophic consequences (for the full story, see *The Cretaceous Times*).

Meteor Crater (above) is 4,150 feet across and 570 feet deep. Scientists calculate that a 63,000-ton nickel-iron rock the size of a small house crashed to earth about 50,000 years ago to blast this enormous hole in the northern Arizona desert.

This "eye-witness" report of what followed from a cosmic collision between Earth and an asteriod some 66.4 million years ago is based on current scientific evidence and theory.

THE CRETACEOUS TIMES

Final Edition   March 8, 66,400,000 BC

DOOMSDAY ASTEROID COLLIDES WITH EARTH

By Mari N. Jensen

Chicxulub, Mexico (66.4 million years BC)

A fiery 6-mile-wide asteroid with a glowing tail plummeted into the continental shelf by Mexico's Yucatan Peninsula, vaporizing rocks and water and making a crater 112 miles wide. The scientific community predicts cataclysmic consequences for life on earth.

Globules of molten rock and clouds of sulfur dust are rising high into the atmosphere. As the tiny superheated pellets of rock fall back to earth like hot hail stones, forests around the world are bursting into flames, creating a death-dealing firestorm.

The whole world may catch fire, predict scientists.

And, although rain may fall, the sulfur dust kicked up by the asteroid's impact will turn that rain into a shower of sulfuric acid. As the acid rain drains into rivers and oceans, the change in water chemistry will kill many aquatic plants and animals.

Clouds of smoke and ash are boiling into the skies from the forest fires, making it impossible to see the sun. Meteorologists

say the thick cloud layers of ash and sulfur dust may darken the skies for years. Those dark clouds may block the sun's rays so completely that plants that survive the fires will still die from lack of sunlight.

If that happens, life as we know it in the Cretaceous period would come to an abrupt end. Biologists predict most animals, from the majestic to the miniature, including the dinosaurs, will perish.

Rodents Pulling Your Tail?

Volcanic Necks + Dikes

BENEATH EVERY VOLCANO LIES a labyrinth of channels and chambers through which magma reaches the surface. When a volcano dies, the molten rock inside cools and solidifies. Over time, as erosion eats away at the cone, strange craggy peaks and walls of hardened volcanic rock emerge from the underworld.

In the Four Corners area—where Utah, Arizona, Colorado, and New Mexico meet—travelers can see more than 100 dark, jagged, seemingly out-of-place landforms jutting up from the flats. These **volcanic plugs**, or **necks** as they are called, are the hardened remains of molten rock that once plugged the throats of ancient volcanoes. The Southwest's most famous volcanic neck, Shiprock, rises 1,800 feet (549 m) from the plains of northwestern New Mexico like a ship above the ocean. In Navajo legend, Shiprock is *Sa-bit-tai-e,* the *rock with wings,* a great bird that brought people to this land from the north. In another version, the Twin War Gods, great heroes of the Navajo, killed giants that inhabited the area long ago; Shiprock is the proof—the congealed blood of those giants.

Travelers can also see three prominent walls or wings of volcanic rock, called **dikes,** marching out across the grasslands from Shiprock. The longest dike extends for 5 miles (8 km). When the volcano was alive, the force of explosive eruptions fractured the surrounding bedrock; and these radiating fissures filled with molten lava. Their exposed remains cut vertically through horizontal layers of rock, like a knife stuck in a layer cake. Because the volcanic rock is harder than the soft shale that once encased it, these mysterious features have remained standing long after the rest has worn away.

If you bury a bottle in a pile of sand, as rain flattens the pile and washes sand away, the bottle will eventually reappear. This, in a nutshell, explains why we now see Shiprock (right) and the lava walls that radiate from it (top right) as dramatic, seemingly out-of-place features in the flat land around them.

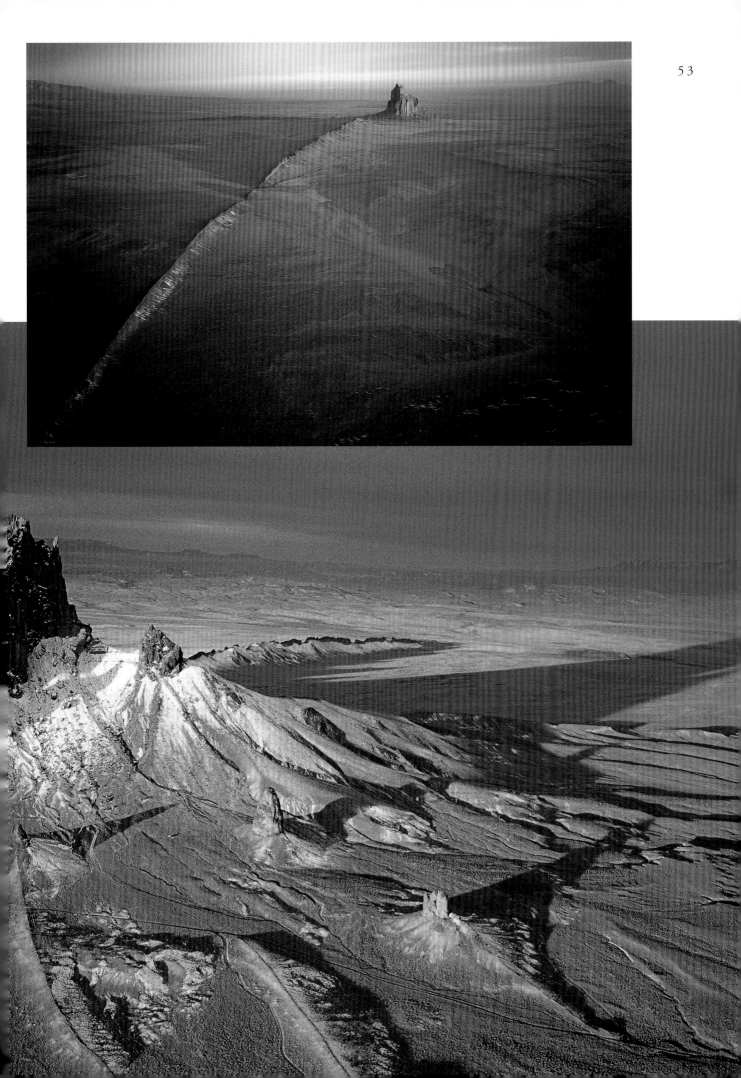

Standing Up

Shapes

"Wherever we look there is but a wilderness of rocks . . . and ten thousand strangely carved forms in every direction. . ." JOHN WESLEY POWELL

STANDING STONES, sacred and mysterious as the ring of Stonehenge, speak volumes to those who stand before them. People journey to the Southwest to behold the raw majesty of rock, in infinite variations of color, texture, and form. What might seem to be the work of some supernatural artist—from graceful arches and awesome cliffs to replicas of Pancho Villa and Queen Victoria—all were created by the simple forces of weathering.

Full moon rising over Monument Valley, Arizona (left). Above, a fanciful silhouette in Bryce Canyon National Park, Utah: Pluto?

The work of water, wind, living organisms, and changing temperature reduces rocks to sand and soil. In arid lands—where soils are thin and vegetation sparse—the principle weathering tools are physical, but they work in tandem with chemical weathering. Moisture runs into cracks and expands as it freezes, wedging rocks apart. Plant roots penetrate and pry. Water and weak organic acids from rotting leaves dissolve minerals that glue rocks together. Thin shells of rock flake away from the surface, much like an onion peel, a process called **exfoliation**. And, as moisture seeps below ground, softer rocks and minerals decompose. Even hard granite eventually decays to clay and granules of quartz.

Rock loosened by the slow devices of weathering is whisked away by flash floods, the power-house of desert ero-sion. Within minutes, a summer thunderstorm can fill a previously dry wash with a wall of water ten feet high. Though infrequent and short-lived, desert downpours can clear canyons and level mountains.

Over eons, forces that formed the shapes we see in the rock today will sculpt new ones. Dramatic pinnacles, cliffs, and arches are inspir-ing reminders that weathering is more than a destructive force—it is a creative one.

WEATHERING

Freezing, thawing—soaking, drying—heating, cooling—all help to break rocks down. Sheets of granite flake away from the surface (above) and gradually decompose to gravel, allowing plants such as pussypaws to gain a foothold (top left). Death Valley monkeyflowers (bottom left) invade a crack in a canyon wall—they, too, will alter rocks both physically and chemically.

Snow graces the amphitheater at Bryce Canyon National Park (bottom right) and a canyon wall near Sedona, Arizona (top right).Though beautiful to behold, ice is the chief destroyer of rocks in this red rock country.

Mesas, Buttes + Pinnacles

IN A LAND where shallow seas and dune fields once stretched to the horizon, steep-sided table-lands and soaring spires now reach for the sky like outlaws in a western movie. Aptly enough, Monument Valley, a central player in this south-western drama, has served as the backdrop for numerous films, from *Stagecoach* to *Indiana Jones and the Last Crusade.* But the directors of this exquisite earth-scene were time itself and the powerful forces of weathering and erosion.

Monument Valley, along the Arizona-Utah border, provides an unparalleled assortment of gorgeous red plateaus (French for *trays*), mesas (Spanish for *tables*), and buttes (French for *hills*). The vast, elevated expanses of land called **plateaus** are bordered on at least one side by steep cliffs. Some, such as the Colorado Plateau, have been intricately dissected by canyons into smaller plateaus. Discrete, flat-topped remnants of a plateau that rise above the surrounding plain or valley floor are called **mesas**. They maintain this shape because a mesa's tabletop, the cap rock, is more resistant to erosion than the rocks beneath. But mesas do weaken around the edges, and through undercutting, rock continues to fracture and fall. Chunks of fallen rock, **talus**, pile up below.

As erosion continues, a mesa will eventually become a **butte** when it is no longer wider than it is tall. As it shrinks further, it becomes a slender stone monument, a **spire** or **pinnacle**, such as Monument Valley's famous Totem Pole, the spire Clint Eastwood used for climbing practice in *The Eiger Sanction.* These stone sentinels, too, will crumble someday, and join the rippling red sand on the valley floor.

In an attempt to help the Navajo people during the Great Depression, Harry and Leone "Mike" Goulding—compassionate folks who operated a trading post in Monument Valley—drove to Hollywood to capture the attention of Western film producer John Ford. Armed with scenic photographs and persistence, they succeeded; and Monument Valley (above) became John Ford's favorite movie location. One promising actor under his direction, John Wayne (right, seen with Harry Carey, Jr. in *The Searchers*), starred in five legendary films shot there between 1939 and 1956.

Hopi: Heard Museum Phoenix
Pueblo Art USA 13c

Acoma: School of American Research
Pueblo Art USA 13c

MESA-TOP ATTRACTIONS

ROOMS WITH A VIEW

Three mesas in north-central Arizona—First, Second, and Third—are home to the Hopi people. Established around A.D. 1200 on Third Mesa, Oraibi is the oldest continually inhabited town in the United States. Travelers should plan to visit the Hopi Cultural Center on Second Mesa before heading to Walpi, an ancient adobe village perched high atop First Mesa. Tours of this ancient village can be arranged on-site, but no photography is permitted.

Acoma Pueblo sits atop a fortress-like sandstone mesa in northwestern New Mexico. It was the subject of Willa Cather's short story "The Enchanted Bluff," and figured prominently in her novel DEATH COMES TO THE ARCHBISHOP. *In 1599, to punish the Acoma who had withheld supplies, Spanish colonists stormed and destroyed Acoma Pueblo and most of its people. Today, tourists are permitted to visit Acoma when accompanied by a tribal guide, which is easy to arrange at a roadside stop at the foot of the mesa. Photography is not permitted.*

(DRAMATIC MUSIC THROUGHOUT)
ANNCR: (VO) It's here.

A typewriter superior to the IBM
Electronic 75.

Even IBM admits this is better
than their best electronic typewriter.

What could possibly be better than the
IBM Electronic 75?

SECRETARY: Why, the IBM Electronic 85,
what else?

DELIVERY BOY: (HUFF, PUFF) Tuna on
rye, no pickle.
SECRETARY: That was tuna on white.

TWO FAMOUS PINNACLES

According to Navajo legend, Spider Woman lives at Spider Rock, an 800-foot (244-m) spire rising from the floor of Canyon de Chelly, Arizona (right). It's said that Spider Woman taught the region's native people how to weave.

For eye-catching advertisements, cars, grand pianos, even a secretary at her desk have been transported by helicopter to the tiny top of Totem Pole (left), a slender pinnacle in Monument Valley on the Utah-Arizona border. While only 14 feet (4.3 m) wide, this pinnacle stands 300 feet (91 m) tall.

PEAK PERFORMANCE

Advertisers can't seem to get enough of Totem Pole (left), the pinnacle used in 1983 for a 30-second commercial by the Doyle Dane Bernbach advertising firm. A stuntwoman "secretary" was transported with desk to Totem Pole's tiny top to announce the arrival of state-of-the art word processing technology, the IBM Electronic 85 typewriter. Six panels from the storyboard appear above, courtesy of IBM. Climbing Totem Pole is no longer permitted.

Beginning with its lure to the Hollywood film industry back in the 1930s, Monument Valley (left) has been an important source of revenue for the Navajo. And the tradition continues today through tourism, movie-making, and commercial advertising shoots. The Monument Valley Tribal Park, established in 1958, straddles the Arizona-Utah border and encompasses much of the valley's famous awe-inspiring scenery.

Hoodoos

IN PAIUTE MYTHOLOGY, hoodoos are Legend People that Coyote froze in stone as punishment for laughing at him. On moonlit nights, if you stand on the rim of Bryce Canyon, you can hear the hoodoos laughing still . . . or is it the wind?

A **hoodoo** is a bit of erosional whimsy—any irregularly shaped pillar of stone or odd-shaped rock with parts that have weathered away in uneven ways. Where rock layers of different hardness are exposed to the elements—as in the colorful amphitheaters at Bryce Canyon and Cedar Breaks—the softer parts crumble more quickly than the resistant layers. This process of **differential erosion** creates hoodoos. Your imagination can run wild among exotic landforms in the Southwest—you just might see goblins and trolls, owls and elephants, wizened witches and dancing sirens.

In general form, hoodoos vary greatly from place to place, depending upon the parent rock. In the Jemez Mountains of New Mexico, soft, gray volcanic **tuff** (cemented ash) weathers into wigwam shapes. Where tuff is harder, as in New Mexico's City of Rocks State Park, you might see a gathering of old women, their shoulders hunched against the cold. In Arizona's Chiricahua National Monument, you'll see galleries of sturdy tuff columns and massive balanced rocks. The equally enormous, granitic hoodoos in Joshua Tree National Park, California, assume smoother, more curvaceous forms. And in the heart of hoodooland—the Colorado Plateau—intricately layered landscapes of colorful sandstone, limestone, clay, and mudstone give rise to some of the most delicate, picturesque, and fanciful shapes in nature.

So pack your imagination along with your clothes . . . and remember never to laugh at Coyote.

FANTASY FORMS

Story-book characters emerge from a weathering wall of sandstone in Utah's Goblin Valley State Park (opposite, top). Because some portions of the rock are softer than others, surfaces weather at different rates, creating sculptures of time. Those still standing have watched their softer cousins dissolve into loose sand (above and below, also in Goblin Valley). Hardened tuff rocks in Chiricahua National Monument weather into more massive forms (opposite, bottom).

Cliffs + Alcoves

TUCKED under the rim-rock of Mesa Verde and Canyon de Chelly are silent villages built of stone. Ancient Pueblo people (the Anasazi) lived here until unknown events—perhaps drought, famine, or human competition—drove them from their rocky retreats.

How were the sheer rock walls that first beckoned these cliff-dwellers formed? When the whole Colorado Plateau began to rise about 10 million years ago, gravity forced rivers and streams crossing the region to cut harder and faster. Keeping pace with the uplift, canyons were born. As rivers sliced through different types of bedrock, canyon walls took shape (see Canyons).

In open landscapes beyond the confines of canyons, other cliffs march for miles across the plateau country. Their origins differ and are complex—some involved shifts along deeply buried faults—but all represent hard layers of rock that persisted while erosion stripped away softer rock above and around them. In Grand Staircase-Escalante National Monument, giant tilted terraces and cliffs climb from a plateau along the North Rim of the Grand Canyon to even higher plateaus to the west and north. These colorful cliffs bear names that suit them—Chocolate, Vermilion, White, Gray, and Pink. And they have eroded in stair-step fashion to create the Grand Staircase that leads up to the Pink Cliffs, gloriously exposed at Bryce and Cedar Breaks.

GIANT STEPS + CLIFF HOUSES

The land across southwestern Utah has eroded into a step-like series of plateaus and colorful cliffs that march from the Grand Canyon north across Grand Staircase-Escalante National Monument. The top of the staircase—edged by the Pink Cliffs—is beautifully exposed in the amphitheaters of Cedar Breaks National Monument (opposite, right) and Bryce Canyon National Park.

Throughout the Colorado Plateau region, early Native Americans settled along rivers, many in canyons. They often constructed small shelters and storage bins within natural alcoves in cliff faces. Hundreds of these reminders of the past dot the region occupied by ancestral Pueblo peoples and their predecessors (see map, page 69).

In central Arizona, by the Verde River, the Sinagua people built an impressive high-rise cliff house within a natural limestone alcove (above), the main feature of Montezuma Castle National Monument.

In Mesa Verde National Park (see map, page 69), 23 prehistoric Indian sites are open to the public. Most were built on mesa-tops, but around A.D. 1200, Pueblo people moved to the canyons and built elaborate dwellings in cliffside alcoves. Some—like Oak Tree House (left)—were relatively simple, while others contained more than 100 rooms.

OVERLEAF ▶

Junction Ruin in Canyon de Chelly was built more than 700 years ago.

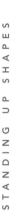

Square Tower House (left), one of Mesa Verde's architectural masterpieces, is an 80-room complex with a tower four-stories high. Its only access was by hand and toe holes hammered into the sandstone cliff face.

Cliff dwellers who settled in what is now Bandelier National Monument enlarged natural cavities in the soft canyon walls that were riddled with holes like Swiss cheese (below).

The shallow, cave-like **alcoves** that prehistoric cliff dwellers called home are for the most part natural features. They form when water seeping downward through a porous layer of rock—often sandstone—meets another layer of rock that resists the flow, forcing the water to move sideways until it reaches the canyon wall. Over time, where the two layers meet, stone begins to weaken, crack, and fall away, forming an alcove. Cliff dwellers reinforced these natural shelters high above the canyon floors with rocks and timbers collected nearby.

While these early Pueblo people in Colorado and Arizona were busy filling natural sandstone alcoves with dwellings of elaborate design—most notably those seen today in Mesa Verde National Park, Navajo National Monument, and Canyon de Chelly—their cousins in New Mexico's Frijoles Canyon faced a bigger challenge. Although they found numerous hollows in the canyon walls, most were too small to be of much use. The compressed volcanic ash (tuff) that formed these cliffs is relatively soft, and, by using harder stone for tools, these industrious people

were able to gouge out shelters and ceremonial chambers (kivas). Many of the lower alcoves functioned as back rooms in houses built against the cliff face. Their accomplishments are showcased at Bandelier National Monument.

Curiously, the prehistoric farmers who built spectacular cliff houses on the Colorado Plateau occupied them for less than a century. Many of their other buildings—on exposed mesas and canyon floors—have disintegrated. But the cliff dwellings, so well protected from the elements, stand today in mute homage to early civilizations.

The five major groupings of prehistoric peoples shown on this map are still being debated among archeologists—there were cultural differences within each group and much exchange took place between them. Only the Hohokam—who farmed open country in Sonoran Desert river basins—never built cliff houses. But even amongst the others, most settlements were kept out in the open. Mogollon (*MUGGY-own*) peoples occupied the largest region of the Southwest, and their most famous cliff dwelling can be explored in Gila Cliff Dwellings National Monument (below).

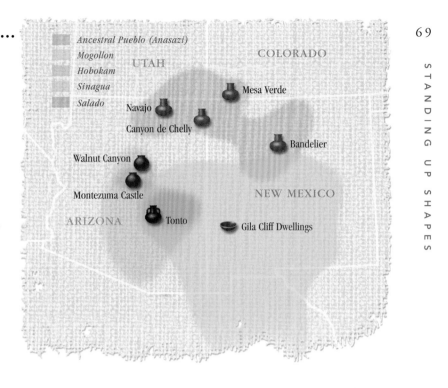

Ancestral Pueblo (Anasazi)
Mogollon
Hohokam
Sinagua
Salado

UTAH
COLORADO

Mesa Verde
Navajo
Canyon de Chelly
Bandelier
Walnut Canyon
Montezuma Castle
NEW MEXICO
ARIZONA
Tonto
Gila Cliff Dwellings

MAJOR CLIFF DWELLINGS

Arches + Bridges

THERE ARE SACRED PLACES in the plateau country where rainbows are captured in stone. That is as it should be, for the Navajo who live nearby believe that the gods travel on the arching back of the rainbow goddess. Natural bridges and arches stand as tribute to the strength of rock, to the shaping forces of weathering and erosion—and to the rainbow goddess.

Bridges span watercourses—running streams or arroyos that carry intermittent runoff. On the Colorado Plateau, rivers meander along canyon bottoms and sometimes double back on themselves. Bridges develop where these winding waterways take a shortcut and eat their way through a solid wall of rock (see illustration). Weathering finishes the job, gently rounding rough edges and smoothing contours into the graceful shapes now seen in some of the older spans—Rainbow Bridge and Sipapu Bridge are superb examples.

Rainbow Bridge (left)
and Sipapu Bridge
(above).

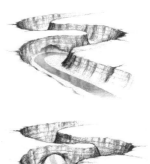

**THE MAKING
OF A NATURAL
BRIDGE**
From a shallow,
meandering stream
(right, top) to canyon
formation (middle) and
a stream-cut hole
through a narrow
canyon wall

Illustrations by David Fischer

FAMOUS NATURAL BRIDGES

Rainbow Bridge (top left), the world's largest natural bridge, spans 275 feet (84 m) and soars 290 feet (88 m) above the floor of Bridge Canyon in Utah's Rainbow Bridge National Monument. This park shares a boundary with Glen Canyon National Recreation Area and the Navajo Nation and can be easily reached by boat across Lake Powell .

Three other stunning bridges—Sipapu (top right), Kachina, and Owachoma—can be seen by car or explored on foot in Utah's Natural Bridges National Monument.

Arches, on the other hand, do not span watercourses and are the work of weathering from start to finish. They are more abundant than bridges and may be as small as a door or as large as a highway overpass. Arches form in many types of rock, but in the Southwest they are best developed in weathered sandstone cliffs and outcrops on the Colorado Plateau.

It's no geological accident that the Colorado Plateau has the largest showcase of natural arches in the world, concentrated in Arches and Canyonlands National Parks. Roughly 300 million years ago, a warm shallow sea occupied most of southern Utah. As the climate changed, the sea shrank, evaporated, and left behind a thick bed of salt. Over eons that followed, intervals of flooding and filling covered the salt with layers of silt and sand, heavy deposits that would eventually cement into place as stone.

When squeezed, salt begins to liquefy and move; and beneath what is now Arches National Park, the salt shifted and, in places, pushed towards the surface. This pressure from below caused the overlying sandstone to dome up and crack into long blocks. These fractures (**joints** to the geologist) have eroded into narrow canyons divided by tall, thin slabs of stone called **fins**. As rainwater and ice weakened the cements holding sandstone together, pieces of the fin would break away, forming pits and alcoves. Some enlarged into unfinished, **blind arches**, similar to those seen in cliffs at Zion National Park; others broke through as small **windows**. Continued weathering has shaped a few of these openings into the delicate and grandiose arches we see today (see illustration).

As new arches and bridges form, the older and grander ones will eventually fall. But most of the delicate stone spans that grace the plateau will certainly outlive our fragile frames.

arch

fins   joints

From the air, much of Arches National Park looks striped—the rocky landscape is fractured into long, narrow, parallel panels. Along the exposed edges, weathering widens the cracks (joints) between them (left). As weathering continues, the panels shrink to become thin walls of rock—fins—and when weak spots break through, a tiny window appears (far left). Those that grow larger without collapsing form arches. The one in the circle is Window Rock, namesake of the Tribal Headquarters of the Navajo Nation.

Illustrations by Leo Galbadon and David Fischer

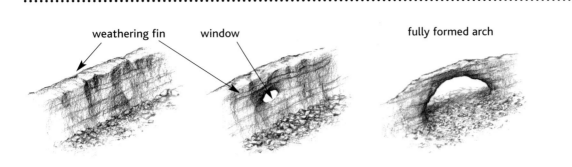

weathering fin

window

fully formed arch

STAGES IN THE FORMATION OF A NATURAL ARCH

ARCHES, ARCHES, + MORE ARCHES

Because of its unique geology, the region occupied by Arches and Canyonlands National Parks is rich in natural arches—the largest concentration in the world. Though Arches has more arches, some of those in Canyonlands are on the fanciful side— Horse Hoof Arch, for example (left).

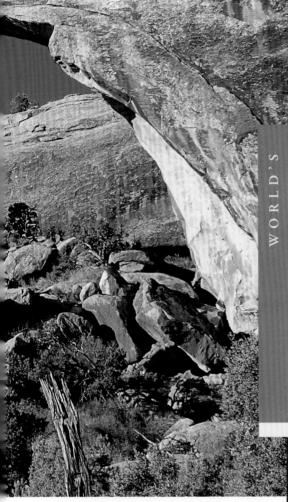

WORLD'S LARGEST ARCH

Two of Utah's national parks are home to the longest natural stone spans in the world—both are about the length of a football field. A visit to Kolob Arch in the backcountry of Zion National Park requires a seven-mile hike, one way. More accessible to travelers is Landscape Arch (left) in Arches National Park.

In 1991, a huge stone slab fell from the underbelly of Landscape Arch, followed by other rockfalls in 1995 and 1996. The trail beneath is now considered dangerous and has been closed. But the whole span can still be seen from the main trail.

Among the main attractions in Arches National Park is free-standing Delicate Arch (left), seen here with the snow-capped La Sal Mountains behind. Reaching this viewpoint requires a rather strenuous 3-mile hike, round-trip (no shade), but it's worth the effort. Another viewpoint, close to the road, offers an interesting but distant view. Turret Arch (above) is on its way to becoming a double arch. And Keyhole Arch (right) is one of several remarkable arches in Monument Valley.

Dunes

"... you have not known what force resides in mindless things until you have known a desert wind." MARY AUSTIN

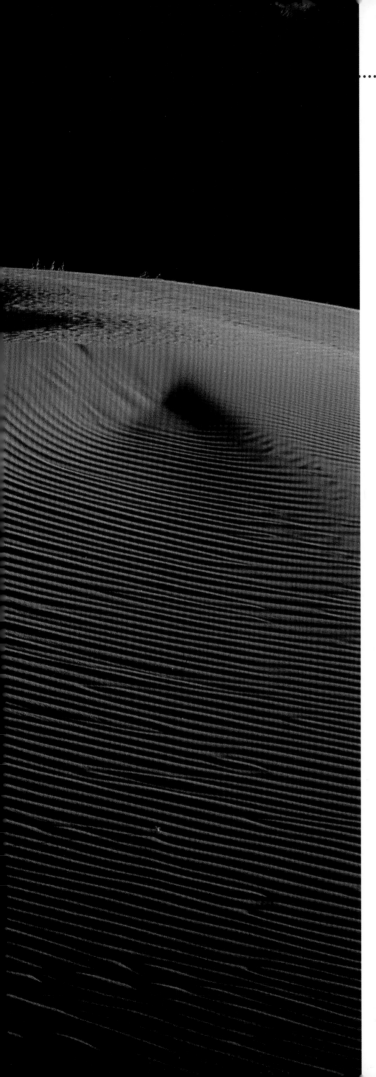

SAND DUNES ARE STARK, sensuous, and alluring. Here you can actually see and feel the earth reshaping itself, in ways that are less dramatic and threatening than volcanoes but no less captivating. Mention the word *desert,* and most people think of dunes. Yet, in all deserts of North America combined, dunes form less than 1% of the landscape.

A small, unnamed dune field in northern Arizona (left). A more familiar one skirts Totem Pole in Monument Valley (above).

REAWAKENING

Over time, cemented sands of prehistoric dunes break free . . . and are on the move again, clearly seen in this aerial view over the western edge of the Moenkopi Plateau in north-central Arizona. On the floor of Canyon de Chelly, weathered mounds of swirling, criss-crossed layers of sandstone echo the shapes of dunes from which they came (far right).

Welch's milkweed (near right) is a sand specialist found nowhere in the world except in Utah's Coral Pink Sand Dunes State Park. It blooms in mid-summer.

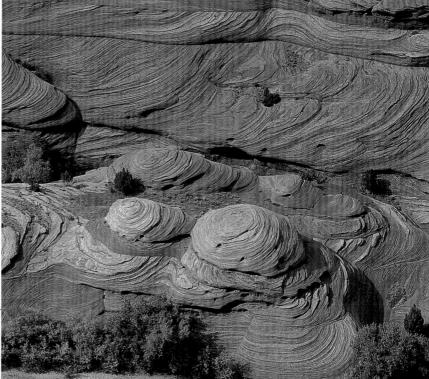

Making a sand dune requires wind, a source of sand, and a place where the shape of the land forces the wind to drop it. In a desert, the wind does not blow any harder than elsewhere, but because water is rare, plants that would slow or stabilize dunes are sparse. Wind can skip or bounce loose sand grains along the desert floor; as grains collide, they jump and roll forward, what geologists call **saltation**. In this manner, most sand travels close to the ground. Wind drives each patch of sand forward until a topographic barrier—a mountain range, for example—brings it to rest. Only a tiny amount of sand (less than 1%) is lofted high into the air, to be carried for perhaps hundreds of miles before settling back down to earth.

There are three sources of dune sand in the Southwest: sand weathered from petrified dunes, sand in river and lake deposits, and sand formed from salt minerals, such as gypsum, that crystallize directly from evaporating lakes.

Across the Colorado Plateau, pre-served in the rounded contours of golden and pink-hued sandstones, are ancient dunes that tell of a time when the region was even more arid than today, similar perhaps to the Sahara Desert. About 170 million years ago, these dunes were buried and cemented into place by solutions of minerals that percolated down between the sand grains. Today, weathering releases ancient quartz sand from these petrified dunes to be reworked and sculpted by the wind. Thus, the same sandstone formation that defines Rainbow Bridge and the cliffs of Zion provides the raw material for Coral Pink Sand Dunes State Park in southern Utah.

FROZEN IN TIME

Checkerboard Mesa (above)—a scenic icon in Zion National Park—is a prehistoric mountain of sand frozen in time. Weathering is at work on its exposed, checkered face, where shallow, vertical cracks in the rock—thought to be made by surface heating and cooling—meet horizontal cracks between layered beds of sandstone.

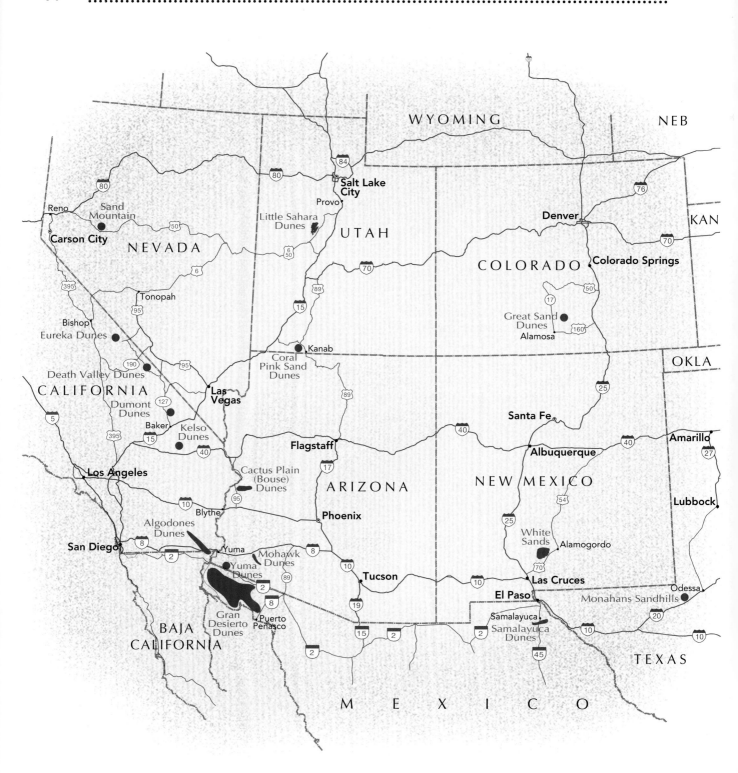

MAJOR DUNE FIELDS

Note: circles represent those with an area under 50 sq mi (130 sq km)

Most of the active dune fields in the Southwest get their sand from ancient river and lake deposits. Great Sand Dunes National Monument in Colorado, for example, probably began to form about 12,000 years ago as glaciers retreated from the Rocky Mountain region. The Rio Grande, swollen with glacial melt and debris, spread sand and gravel across a large portion of the San Luis Valley. The process continues today as prevailing westerly winds sweep across the valley floor, propelling the sand toward the Sangre de Cristo Mountains, where it comes to rest. Strong easterly winds and moisture help to confine the dunes and hold them in place. Unable to migrate, these towering dunes can only grow higher and higher. Cresting at 750 feet (230 m), these are the tallest dunes in North America.

The Southwest's most astonishing sand dunes, composed entirely of sugary white **gypsum**, can be seen at White Sands National Monument, New Mexico. Gypsum is a common mineral in the surrounding mountains. Like salt, gypsum dissolves in water, and, in solution, flows into the water table and lake basins below. As this mineral-rich water evaporates in the dry desert air, gypsum crystallizes, and weathering reduces these crystals to sand-sized bits. Wind then transports the sand from dry lake basins to the dune field.

Sand dunes can exist for thousands of years, maintaining their elegant form as they creep silently over the desert floor.

White Sands is the largest gypsum dune field in the world. Gypsum crystals (top)—some as long as your arm—form in a nearby lake bed and wind carries sand-sized particles into the dune field. Drifting sand encroaches on a soaptree yucca (below)—it will respond by growing faster to keep from being buried alive.

Dune Fields + Forms

THE SHAPE OF A DUNE DEPENDS upon the direction of the prevailing winds. Dunes have two slopes or "faces." The windward face has a gradual slope. Sand blown from the windward face is deposited on the steeply sloping leeward or "slip" face. Curiously, when the slipface reaches an angle of 30-34°, sand always begins to avalanche.

The small but alluring Eureka Dune field (below)—backed by the Last Chance Mountain Range—lies within Death Valley National Park near its northwestern boundary. Sand drifted here from the bed of an Ice Age lake. Stabilized hummocks of thorny dalea occupy this portion of the dune field, and Eureka is closed to all off-road vehicles.

AND FORMS

CRESCENT DUNES
In the heart of an inland dunefield one can find crescent-shaped dunes with their noses aimed into the wind and arms pointing downwind. These are also called **barchan dunes**. Barchans occur in open areas with a uniform wind direction, as in New Mexico's White Sands National Monument, Colorado's Great Sand Dunes National Monument, and much of Mexico's Gran Desierto. They may travel quickly—more than 330 feet (100 m) in a year.

U-SHAPED, OR PARABOLIC DUNES
Where vegetation stabilizes the sand near the edges of dune fields, U-shaped dunes form. Plants anchor their elongated, trailing arms as the bulk of the sand noses forward. These **parabolic dunes** are common in coastal dune fields, but also occur inland—in White Sands National Monument, in the Kelso dune field, and at Coral Pink Sand Dunes State Reserve, for example. They are also the slowest moving dunes, crawling less than eight feet annually.

TRANSVERSE DUNES
These long, somewhat wavy sand ridges form at right angles to the strongest wind direction. They occur in areas of abundant sand and appear to represent lines of coalesced crescent dunes. White Sands National Monument has many transverse dunes, as do Death Valley, the Algodones dune field, and Great Sand Dunes National Monument.

STAR DUNES
Strong winds that blow from multiple directions create star-shaped dunes that tend to remain fixed in one place. They are often higher than other dune forms. Star dunes occur in Great Sand Dunes National Monument, Death Valley, White Sands National Monument, and the Gran Desierto of northwestern Mexico.

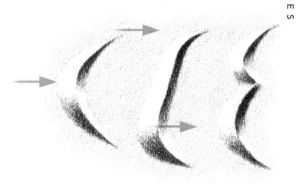

CRESCENT

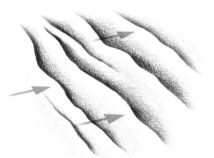

TRANSVERSE

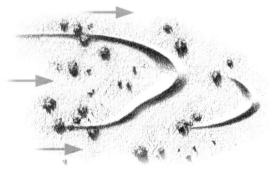

U-SHAPED

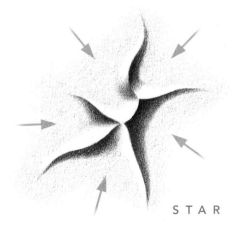

STAR

Illustrations by David Fischer

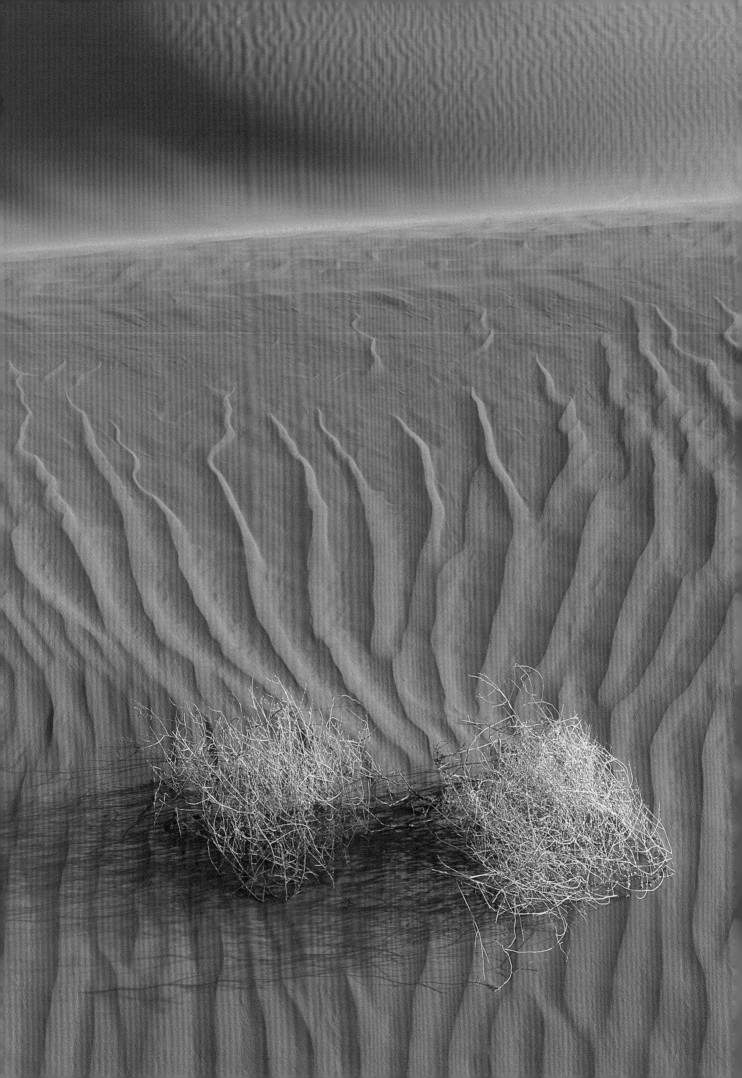

Surviving in Sand

Skeletons of desert dicoria (opposite) and long-leaf sunflower (right) speak of the struggle to survive in shifting sand.

SAND DUNES ARE NOT FOR THE WEAK—they are ruled by extremes. Hot days, cold nights, and wild swings in temperature are the norm. Wind-driven sand buries plants and tears at their parts. Dry desert air sucks moisture from their leaves. Sunrays bombard tender tissues from above and bounce off the sand to strike from below. And dunes are nutrient-poor, not a fertile place to call home.

Lured by prospects of catching sight of a jackrabbit or hearing sand sing, the photographer made this trek across the Eureka Dunes (left).

MUSICAL DUNES

For centuries, travelers through sand seas have recounted tales of singing or booming dunes. On a hot, dry day in a dune field, you, too, might hear them. Singing sand has been documented in the American Southwest in four places: Sand Mountain, Nevada; Great Sand Dunes National Monument, Colorado; and Kelso Dunes and Eureka Dunes in California.

On a hot, dry day, climb to the crest of a dune and slide down the steep slip face—as avalanching sand vibrates, you might hear a droning roar. Exactly why dunes boom or sing when the sand slides no one knows, except that grains of musical dunes are smoother than ordinary sand particles.

Dune plants are superbly adapted to cope with their severe and constantly changing world. Leaves and stems are often covered with silvery fuzz, helping to shield the plant from sunburn. Most avoid extremes by settling between or around the edges of the active dunes, where the wind is milder and the sand more stable. Others are better prepared for life in shifting sand. When sand engulfs the soaptree yucca, it grows faster. An old yucca plant can be 40 feet (12 m) tall, buried up to its neck, with only a bundle of leaves and a plume of white flowers poking out.

Like the yucca, squawbush (also called skunkbush sumac, prominent in White Sands National Monument) can hasten its growth to stay above encroaching sand; but, unlike the yucca, this shrub has an extensive root mass. Roots that sprout along the length of its buried stems clutch a wide column of sand. As a dune begins to move away and wind threatens to undercut the plant, the squawbush remains secure, sitting high atop its pedestal of hardened, erosion-resistant sand—an odd sight, like a ship out of water, stranded until the next dune arrives.

Brilliant wildflowers, and even insects that feed upon them, know when to lie low and when to spring into action. Seeds may tumble in the wind and shifting sand for years before finding ideal conditions for germination. But when the time is right, seedlings take root and bloom at a frantic pace. They must. The slow ones might be buried alive, dry up, or be eaten by insects before setting seed. Fortunately, sand soaks up moisture quickly and retains it well. In a good year, a single purple sand verbena may have enough time to spread into a flower-studded mat more than ten feet across, helping to stabilize the dunes, temporarily.

SURVIVAL TACTICS

Odd sight that it is, a giant sand pedestal rises from an active dune field in White Sands National Monument (above). The root mass of this squawbush has literally "held its ground" as wind stripped away the dune from around it. A yucca clinging to the side of the pedestal—front center—has lost most of its footing and will probably die before the next dune settles in.

Other plants, the desert annuals, must grow, flower, and set seed in a flash. White desert primrose (opposite, top) and purple sand verbena (opposite, bottom) are among the most fragrant and best adapted to dunes in the Sonoran Desert.

Animals have an advantage—they can move to avoid the harshest conditions. Most are active only at night or during the cool twilight hours. To discover the richness of unseen animal life, walk a dune field at daybreak—the sand will be scored with mysterious holes and tracks. Common residents are foxes, coyotes, badgers, rabbits, mice, birds, lizards, snakes, spiders, and a multitude of insects. Many live in burrows that offer shelter from temperature extremes at the surface—just one foot down, the sand remains a tolerable temperature day and night.

Some dune-dwellers are sand specialists. Side-winding rattlesnakes are equipped with an unusual form of locomotion, enabling them to slide efficiently over loose sand. The fringe-toed lizard of the Mojave and Sonoran deserts has comb-like scales on the edges of its toes, which keep the lizard from sinking into the sand when it runs. They have been clocked at over 20 miles per hour (34 km/hr). What the lizard can't outrun, it

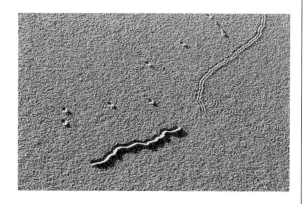

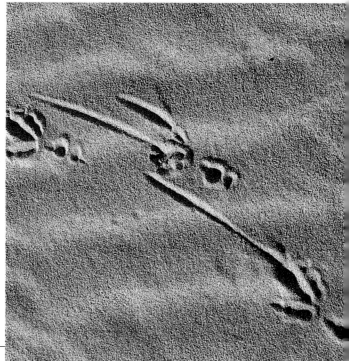

escapes by swimming into the sand. Specialized eyelids and earflaps protect its eyes and ear openings. The list of adaptations goes on and on.

From a distance, dunes seem as stark and barren as the moon. Yet they support a unique community of life that's as strong as the desert wind itself.

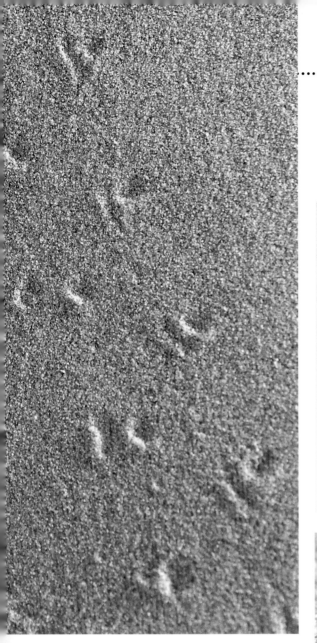

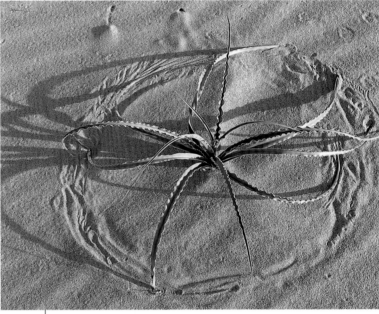

MORE TO LIFE THAN MEETS THE EYE

Dunes are alive with animals, ranging from sand specialists like the fringe-toed lizard (opposite, upper left) and those that tunnel beneath the sand (opposite, bottom left) to generalists like ravens (opposite, bottom right). Insects abound, and caterpillars (top center) can dig underground to escape the hot, dry air and prepare for metamorphosis. Even plants—this ajo lily, for example (top right)—leave tracks in the sand.

DESERT ACROBAT

The darkling beetle (above), a common sight in the Southwest, leaves delicate footprints on the sand as it scurries across the dunes with a stiff-legged gait. This beetle can't fly; its wings are sealed in place over a chamber that works as a heating and cooling system.

People of northwestern Mexico know this critter as the Pinacate beetle, a name linked to the region's dark, Pinacate volcanic field.

PINACATE *is probably derived from the Aztec word for this insect,* PINACATL. *Curiously, the beetle's habit of pausing to point its rear end to the sky suggests the cone of a volcano. This comical headstand posture warns attackers (or curious humans) that it's about to release a foul-smelling spray.*

Deserts on the March

ALTHOUGH DUNES are relatively uncommon worldwide, deserts are not—they cover an area twice the size of the continental United States. Natural deserts are surprising places, pulsing with life and beauty, where only the hardiest survive. Today, deserts are growing unnaturally where plants have been stripped from semi-arid lands for livestock or firewood. Removal of plant life decreases rainfall and allows thin desert soils to be swept away by wind and water, exposing hard, barren rock. As plants become scarce, animal populations dwindle. The Sahara Desert, the largest desert in the world, is growing southward at a rate of three-and-one-half miles a year (5.6 km/yr). Every year, such creeping desertification claims an area the size of Maine.

A GRAPHIC REMINDER

A road divides the Algodones dune field within California's Imperial Sand Dunes Recreation Area. On the south side, off-road vehicles have free access (left, top), while the north side is open to foot traffic only (left, bottom). These photographs were taken on the same day during a springtime bloom of white desert primrose and other wildflowers. Studies show that areas closed to ATV traffic support ten times as many plants as those left open. Apart from the outright destruction of plants, vehicles compact the sand, reducing the amount of water it can store, which inhibits seedling growth.

The Gran Desierto dune field (above) in northwestern Mexico is the largest in North America. This expanse of golden sand flows east from the delta of the lower Colorado River. The world's largest continuous expanse of sand lies in the Empty Quarter of the Arabian Desert, which covers 250,000 square miles, the size of Arizona and New Mexico combined. And the largest sand dunes in the world are in the Sahara— they can be over 1,500 feet (457 m) high.

Water

WHERE

THE SOUTHWEST IS DRY

. . . and there's no telling when the rains will come. To survive, every desert dweller must somehow outwit Nature's fickle deal.

Spadefoot toads are among the champions. They escape the desiccating desert air by slumbering underground ten or more months of the year, only awakening when they feel the rumble of thunder and the pounding of raindrops overhead. In the first summer downpour, they emerge to fill their empty stomachs and mate. Toads spontaneously appear, as if from nowhere, for they've no time to waste. They must get their little ones from eggs to toadlets before puddles dry up—some species can complete the cycle in as little as 11 days. Those that make it dig themselves back into the mud, just as their parents did, and wait in a state of suspended animation for the next rain.

The Sonoran Desert in a summer downpour—the time for spadefoot toads to wake up.

Many desert plants and animals count on summer thunderstorms that come unpredictably and with a vengeance. Wet southerly winds create small, short-lived storm cells of about three miles across. Although a storm's downpour can fill mountain gullies and flood lowlands in a flash, within hours, all that remains for wildlife are ephemeral puddles and ponds.

The desert's fabled spring wildflowers are nourished by winter's gentler rains. Moist air sweeping in off the Pacific Ocean drops much of its moisture as it climbs over California's high Sierra Nevada (Spanish for *snowy mountain range*). Most of the water falls in the mountains as snow, but some slips east over the high ridges and sprinkles Death Valley and the surrounding desert plains. The water drains into dry lake basins, forming shallow reservoirs that host millions of migrating birds. Like the toads, the seeds of desert annuals wait patiently for just the right moisture and temperature conditions, factors that botanists are still endeavoring to understand. A banner-year bloom—seen about once per decade—is a spectacle you'll never forget. Like the frenzied chorus of amorous toads, this explosion of color and perfume allows wildflowers to set seed before all signs of precious moisture have vanished.

DESERTS IN BLOOM

Clockwise from upper left: Ajo lily—Sonoran Desert, Sonora, Mexico. Mojave Desert tapestry of California poppies, goldfields, goldenbush, and Joshua trees—Antelope Valley, California. Lilac sunbonnet—Mojave Desert, California. Male digger bee and sweat bee (tiny) in a desert sunflower—Sonoran Desert, Sonora, Mexico. Desert five-spot—Mojave Desert, Death Valley, California.

Washes + Arroyos

THE GREATER SOUTHWEST has few permanent rivers: foremost are the Colorado, San Juan, Green, Gila, Salt, Virgin, Pecos, and Rio Grande. Feeding these life-giving arteries are networks of smaller drainageways that run intermittently after summer storms, winter rains, and snowmelt (see map, page 118).

GRAND FALLS

During spring snowmelt and after summer storms, the often-dry Little Colorado River rages with muddy water and tumbles over Grand Falls in northern Arizona (right). The falls was born when lava from a volcanic eruption about 100,000 years ago (on the left side of the photograph) dammed the river channel, forcing the water to take a detour over the plateau before dropping back into the gorge.

One of the worst regional floods of the 20th century happened in southern Arizona in October 1983 when tropical storm Octavio dumped six inches of rain in two days. Already saturated from previous rains, the ground had reached its limit. Runoff fed raging rivers of muddy water that ripped out roadways and bridges, swallowed houses, and snapped power lines. Cars, refrigerators, trailers, and parts of houses went swirling downstream as the floodwaters raced through the normally dry riverbeds that wind through the desert metropolis of Tucson.

Since the floods of 1983, an increasing number of southern Arizona's dry riverbeds have been straightened out and their banks stabilized with soil cement. But there's a price to pay for this practice that goes beyond tax dollars. Arroyos act as sponges that help to replenish our vanishing supply of ground water; in straightened drainage channels with cemented banks, water moves faster, has less of a chance to soak in, and raises the risk of erosion and flooding downstream. Southwestern cities must plan to live within the desert's natural rhythms, rather than fight them. Restoring portions of now-dry rivers to their earlier state—that of meandering tree-lined streams—can reduce flooding while maintaining soothing oases for the enjoyment of people and wildlife.

Storm-chaser Thomas Wiewandt films southern Arizona's greatest flood of the last century at the St. Mary's bridge over Tucson's Santa Cruz River channel (right), an arroyo that's usually bone dry. Photo by Gwen Ray.

Dry streambeds or washes are a trademark of desert country. Called **arroyos** (Spanish for *gutter* or *stream*), these dry watercourses have shallow, nearly vertical banks and a U-shaped bottom covered with gravel. Arroyo formation, a process that has been going on for millions of years, can be accelerated by human interference. Many southwestern arroyos developed in the late 19th century, when overgrazing and wood-cutting stripped away vegetation that held soils in place.

After thunderstorms, arroyos fill with the roiling runoff of the storm. As little as six inches of fast-flowing water can sweep a car off the roadway. Every year, television news in the Southwest shows the sad results of attempts to drive through a flooded arroyo. Storm run-off seldom lasts for more than an hour, so it's far better to sit tight for a while than to attempt a risky crossing.

During the summer thunderstorm season, the Southwest sports spectacular waterfalls. Grand Falls on the Little Colorado River, an awesome precipice 185 feet (57m) high, turns from a dry cliff face into a waterfall. Fed by runoff from hundreds of gullies and arroyos, the sometimes dry river careens over the cliff, creating a cataract higher than Niagara Falls.

Watercourse in Death Valley (above)—an arroyo— one that might flow only once or twice a year, but when it does, beware!

Fans + Bajadas

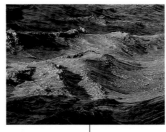

STORM WATER that races from desert mountains drains into washes and then pours into dry valley basins below. As this runoff exits a narrow mountainside canyon, it spreads out, loses speed, and drops its load of sand, gravel, and boulders. With each flooding rain, the pile grows deeper, forming a low fan-shaped deposit called an **alluvial fan**. Alluvial fans are features common to most major mountain ranges in the Southwest.

Death Valley is a showcase for classic alluvial fans. To reach the narrow mouth of the many desert canyons that beckon hikers on the valley floor, you must trudge up an uneven slope of loose rock that has been accumulating for thousands of years. When fans from adjacent canyons merge, the resulting aprons of rocky debris are known as **bajadas** (*bah-HAH-dahs,* Spanish for *slopes*). One that flanks the base of Death Valley's Panamint Mountains is five miles wide and 2,000 feet (610 m) thick in places. In Saguaro

National Park and Organ Pipe Cactus National Monument, rocky terrain high on the bajada slopes supports forests of giant cacti. Closer to the valley floor, however, where finer soils have migrated down-slope, these plants quickly thin out. Among the benefits of rockier soils, these massive cacti can better anchor their extensive but shallow roots, making them less likely to be toppled by wind.

WATER—DESTROYER, BUILDER, GIVER OF LIFE

A fan-shaped heap of out-wash from the Black Mountains meets a seldom-seen carpet of desert sunflowers on the floor of Death Valley (below). Older, more gentle slopes—bajadas—form aprons around most mountain ranges in the Southwest. Saguaro cacti and flowering paloverde trees thrive on these slopes in the Tucson Mountains (right).

Slot Canyons

IN LAS VEGAS, *slots* are those infamous one-arm bandits that rob tourists of spare change. But to locals on the Colorado Plateau, a slot is a dream world of swirling, convoluted canyon walls, a phantasm of sculpted rock dancing in reflected light. The walls, often sunset-hued, are sandstones deposited more than 160 million years ago, when a large Sahara-like desert blanketed the Southwest.

The nearly vertical walls of these fissure-like **slot canyons** were gouged out by water and debris that barreled through them after fierce thunderstorms. What began as a thin crack in the earth widened and deepened as water cut through layers of bedrock. Because slot canyons penetrate rock that is the same type and hardness throughout, the walls tend to erode evenly, producing a chasm of similar width from top to bottom. But, where even slight irregularities exist, floodwaters will strike the walls harder in some places than others, creating hollows that enlarge as swirling water and scouring stones move through them. The outcome is a series of sensuously rounded chambers connected by narrow passages.

Upper Antelope Canyon (right)—a dream world, inner sanctum, holy place—and unfortunately overcrowded. The canyon is short and narrow—just wide enough for one person to squeeze through in spots—so the company of just a dozen visitors feels like a traffic jam. To fully appreciate what a slot canyon can offer, try going there in the off-season—you'll be justly rewarded.

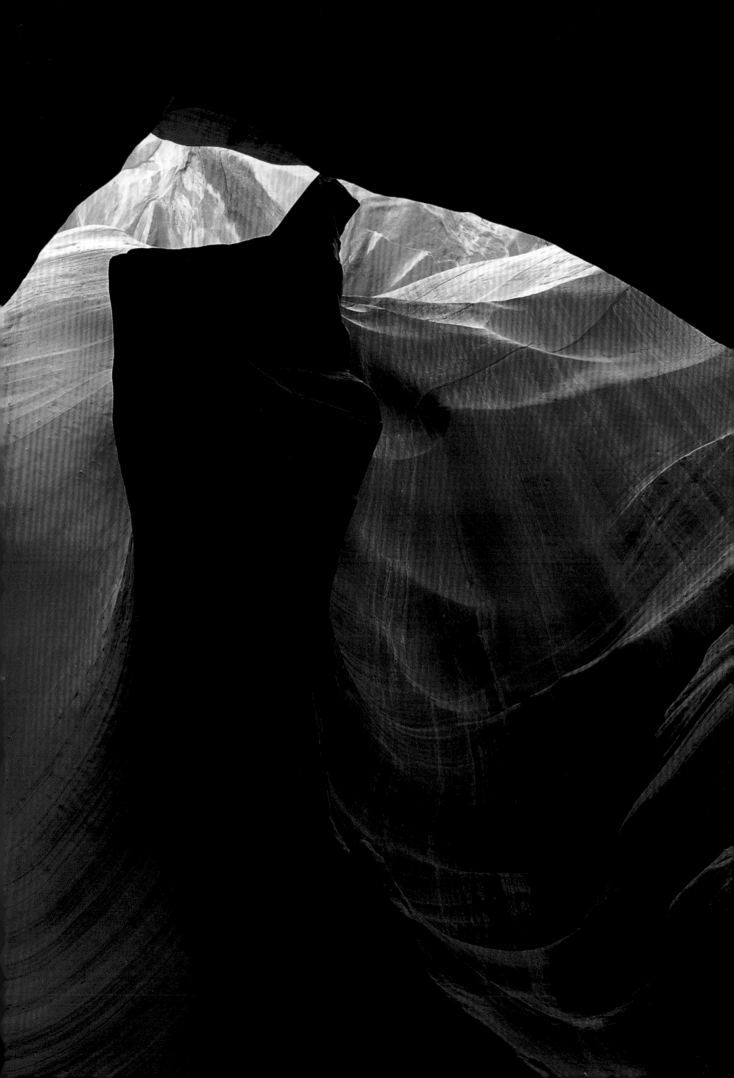

Slot canyons are rare. Most lie along the Colorado River drainage in central and southern Utah and northern Arizona. Some are accessible from Lake Powell; and Antelope Canyon—among the most beautiful—is a short drive from Page, Arizona. Buckskin Gulch, a narrow side canyon to Paria Canyon, is the longest slot canyon in the Southwest, and probably the world. For 12 miles, the canyon's width varies from 3 to 15 ft, and, in places, the walls soar to 400 feet (122 m). The Virgin River Narrows in Zion National Park is among the deepest, a 2,000-foot (610 m) chasm that tapers, in places, to just 30 feet (9 m) in width. And one of the greatest concentrations of slots outside of Las Vegas can be found in the remote Coyote Gulch region of Grand Staircase-Escalante National Monument.

SLOT CANYONS CAN BE DEADLY

In August 1997, a flash flood in northern Arizona's Lower Antelope Canyon swept 11 people to their deaths. Local Navajos warned the out-of-town travelers that afternoon thunderstorms were building on higher slopes eight miles away, but the group entered the canyon against their advice. A rush of floodwater filled the narrow canyon from wall to wall, leaving the hikers no refuge from the deluge. Only one battered survivor emerged from the torrent of mud and debris. Nine of the 11 bodies were found, and the Sheriff's recovery team suspects that the two still missing remain deeply buried.

SLOT CANYON TERRAIN

A slot canyon is deep, narrow, and fissure-like—not a place to get caught when rain comes 'round. Keep in mind that when you're in a slot canyon, your view of the sky will be too restricted for cloud-watching—in the Southwest, storms often mature in less than an hour. An aerial view of typical slot canyon terrain (right, over Grand Staircase-Escalante National Monument) clearly shows how the lay of the land feeds storm runoff into these canyons. This is, in fact, how they were carved.

A canyon entrance near Lake Powell is choked with tumbleweeds (opposite, top) that will quickly be flushed out by the next storm; Below, a summer thunderstorm over the Arizona-Utah border.

WHERE WATER COMES AND GOES

Tanks + Potholes

IN WEST TEXAS, about 30 miles from El Paso, there's an outdoor art gallery inscribed on rocks. The show of some 2,000 paintings spans thousands of years, and among the featured artists are nomadic hunters and gatherers, people of the Mogollon era, Mescalero Apaches, and other Native Americans who camped here. The works—masked figures, animals, abstract symbols, story panels, and more—are lively, colorful, and sophisticated. One recurrent theme seems to be water. In addition to figures resembling the Mesoamerican rain god Tlaloc (above), there are rain clouds, zig-zag patterns (possibly lightning), and pictures that suggest the locations of concealed reservoirs. In fact, it's water, hidden in natural rock basins, that attracted so many diverse people to this spot over the ages. It's all now protected in Hueco Tanks State Historical Park.

FATHER KINO'S TINAJAS

Dozens of tinajas, natural cisterns that can retain thousands of gallons of rainwater year-round, are hidden among the granite peaks of Mexico's Gran Desierto and the adjacent Cabeza Prieta National Wildlife Refuge in Arizona. Jesuit priest Father Eusebio Francisco Kino—scholar, missionary, and early southwestern explorer—was the first to map the locations of these tinajas. Through his knowledge of these remote pockets of water, late in the 17th century he established a lifeline for travelers who crossed the treacherous stretches of the Sonoran Desert between Mexico and California. Such travel disproved the popular notion that California was an island. Ironically, knowledge of his map faded from the record, and, in the 19th century, hundreds of people died of thirst trying to reach California's gold fields. Even today, the whereabouts of these tinajas remains a mystery to most human visitors, though not to bighorn sheep and other desert wildlife that depend on them.

After a summer storm in the desert mountain and plateau country, you're likely to see blue sky reflected in rain-filled depressions. Such **potholes** form when water stands in even the slightest dip in a sandstone, limestone, or granite surface. Water dissolves the cements binding the rock particles together and the loosened particles then blow away or wash away in the next storm, making the depression ever-so-slightly deeper. As the cycle repeats, these cavities deepen, forming potholes an inch deep and a few inches in diameter to sheer-walled cisterns big enough to swallow a bus.

The Waterpocket Fold in Capitol Reef National Park gets its name from the countless potholes—"waterpockets"—scoured in its sandstone terrain. The really big potholes, known as **tanks**, may hold water year-round. In Texas, they are called **huecos** (*WAY-coze*, Spanish for *cavity*). Farther west—in Arizona, California, and Sonora, Mexico—the name **tinajas** (*teen-AH-hahs,* Spanish for *holes*) is most commonly used.

FLEETING WATER

Short-lived supplies of water have always shaped the ways of people and wildlife in the Southwest. Shallow potholes in sandstone on the Colorado Plateau (below) seldom hold rainwater for more than a few days. A desert cottontail (left) pauses to drink while it can.

Playas

THOUGH NAMED **playas** (*PLY-yas,* Spanish for *beaches*), the dry lakes that dot the western deserts in the United States and Mexico don't bring the ocean to mind. Most often, these flat, hardened lakebeds are desolate places that seem better suited for otherworldly adventures like landing the Space Shuttle (at Edwards Air Force Base, California) or setting the world's first supersonic land speed record (in the Black Rock Desert, Nevada).

During the last Ice Age, when the climate was much cooler and wetter, most southwestern playas were filled with water—lakes in landlocked drainage basins between mountain ranges. Even Death Valley once cradled a glistening lake. As the climate warmed to today's temperate conditions, lake water evaporated, leaving dissolved minerals behind. Because storm runoff from nearby mountains transports dissolved salts to lake basins below, playas are often thickly layered with salt deposits.

Although usually seen as bleak, flat, dry landscapes, playas come to life in the rain. Just one desert downpour can cover acres of a dry lakebed with a thin sheet of water—looking for all the world like a mirage. Willcox Playa in southeastern Arizona hosts thousands of sandhill cranes each winter (24,000 during the 1998-99 season). These four-foot-tall birds roost in the shallow water, safe from coyotes and bobcats, and spend their days foraging on leftovers in nearby cornfields. The lake teems with tiny fairy shrimp, food for thousands of smaller wading birds. In February and March, the cranes venture north again, as far as Alaska, to breed. With the approach of summer, the lake vanishes, appearing only as a mirage until the next rain.

Sandhill cranes (left and far right) are winter visitors to playa lakes in Arizona and Texas. Playas can be friendly, but fickle. At top, the X-38 shuttlecraft lands on Rogers Dry Lakebed in southern California. Photo courtesy of NASA

Rainfall retreats from Racetrack Playa in Death Valley National Park, California (right).

WINGS OVER PLAYAS

What do NASA's X-38 spacecraft and sandhill cranes have in common? Both land on playas—the X-38 on Rogers Dry Lakebed in California, and the cranes at Willcox Playa in Arizona and at the Muleshoe playas in Texas.

The X-38 is a prototype for the International Space Station's Crew Return Vehicle (CRV), a "lifeboat" should an emergency arise on the Space Station requiring rapid evacuation of the crew and their return to Earth. Launched from a B-52 carrier aircraft at about 30,000 feet during test flights, the X-38 soars to the ground beneath a steerable red, white, and blue parafoil.

In southeastern Arizona each January, the Willcox Chamber of Commerce sponsors a Wings Over Willcox Sandhill Crane Celebration. The event includes guided birding tours, seminars, and video presentations. When playa lakes at Muleshoe National Wildlife Refuge in western Texas are full, they, too, attract thousands of wintering sandhill cranes. Numbers peak between December and mid-February.

WHAT'S THAT WHITE STUFF?

The hardened, crinkly, lumpy white crust on playa lakes that appears after the water has dried up is mainly salt—sodium chloride—the condiment we sprinkle on our food. Other kinds of salts present include potash (potassium chloride), gypsum (calcium sulfate), and those rich in boron. The kind of salt that crystallizes depends upon the elements dissolved in the water that flows into the playa lake. In Death Valley, the salts (95% table salt) are up to six feet thick. In northern Death Valley, boron-rich fluids have evaporated to produce thick deposits of borates, which have been mined to make glass, fire retardants, and detergents.

The award-winning series Death Valley Days® made broadcast history, running for 35 years, first on radio and then on television, under sponsorship of the Borax Corporation. Audiences worldwide thrilled to stories from the days when teams of 20 mules trudged across Death Valley hauling massive wagons loaded with 12 tons of borax and up to 1,200 gallons of water to keep men and animals alive. To get refined borax out of the valley, mule teams hauled it from Furnace Creek to Mojave, a 165-mile, 10- to 12-day journey. Ronald Reagan starred in the series, along with Clint Eastwood, Carol O'Connor, and actors who became three famous members of the Star Trek Enterprise crew—Spock, Sulu, and Bones. Borax Bill Jr. poster, circa 1905, and photos of Ronald Reagan and of mule team courtesy of U. S. Borax Inc.

HOTTEST PLACE ON EARTH

California's Death Valley is one of the hottest places on Earth, attaining the second-highest temperature ever recorded, 134°F (57°C) on July 10, 1913. Overall, Death Valley is considerably hotter than Al'Aziziyah, Libya, where the official high reached 136°F on September 13, 1922 (although some question the accuracy of this record).

THE WINNER

Under the command of Don Vesco, the Turbinator (above) flashed across Bonneville Salt Flats at 427 mph (687 km/hr) in 1999 to capture the world record for the fastest wheel-driven vehicle of the century.
Photo by Gordon Menzie

FLATTEST AND FASTEST PLACE IN THE WEST

When camels and mastodons roamed the West, one-third of Utah and parts of neighboring states were 980 feet (300 m) under water. This land was at the bottom of ancient Lake Bonneville. All that remains today are its shallow, shrunken remnants: Utah's Great Salt Lake and two huge, seasonally flooded playas, "Lake" Sevier and the Bonneville Salt Flats, covering more than 47 square miles.

Although not as flat, Bolivia's Salar de Uyuni in the Andes is the largest playa in the world, an expanse of salt that covers 3,500 square miles!

Since the start of speed racing on the Bonneville Flats in 1914, hundreds of speed records in a wide variety of automotive and motorcycle classes have been set and broken there. As one racing enthusiast has said on the Internet, "If you're really into imaginatively-

designed race cars driven by people making no-holds-barred speed, this place is home."
Blazing along at 427 miles per hour (687 km/hr), in October 1999, American Don Vesco set this century's record for the world's fastest wheel-driven vehicle. Race competitions are regularly scheduled from August to October, the only season when this playa is predictably dry.

RACING ROCKS

When no one is watching, dozens of stones—even hefty boulders—trek across a desert playa, leaving shallow trails behind. Racetrack Playa in California's Death Valley National Park is famous for its mysterious moving rocks.

Stones tumble down the adjacent mountain slopes and end up on the flat playa floor. Although no one has ever seen one in motion, rocks ranging in size from small cobbles to 700-lb (320-kg) boulders are often found at the ends of what look like tracks etched into the playa's silty surface. The longest continuous track is 1,982 feet (604 m).

How do they do it? One theory holds that wind pushes the rocks along at the rare times when the surface is muddy and slick. Other scientists calculate that to overcome friction, ice must be involved—on a wet, frosty surface, rocks in a strong wind could literally skate across the playa.

Badlands

THE DESOLATE sun-baked landscapes of jagged lava flows, vast dune fields, or blinding salt flats could all be thought of as badlands; certainly hundreds of people have perished trying to cross them. But the word is usually reserved for another kind of terrain that has slowed travelers to a crawl.

The Sioux coined the term *mako sica* (literally *bad land*) to distinguish the barren clay mounds and spires in the Dakotas from the surrounding grassy plains. The term has been adopted by geologists to describe intricately eroded hilly landscapes formed in powdery, clay-rich soils. When it rains, these soft clay slopes erode into a maze of miniature gullies and ridges on steep-sided hills, a challenging terrain to cross on foot or horseback, and almost impossible in a vehicle.

Travelers aren't the only life forms that have trouble in such a landscape. The sponge-like clays absorb rain well but hold the moisture so tightly that few plants can benefit from it. Without roots to help keep the soil in place, erosion is swift. In only ten years, as much as three inches of clay erodes away in Arizona's Painted Desert badlands. At that rate, a hill 25 feet (7.6 m) high would vanish in a thousand years.

On the plus side, speedy erosion of badlands has brought to the surface some of the richest fossil deposits in the world. Fossilized treasure troves of ferns, great coniferous trees, freshwater fishes, amphibians and crocodile-like reptiles scaled to science-fiction proportions, and several kinds of small, early dinosaurs tell us that Petrified Forest National Park once had a climate similar to that in Florida's Everglades. And, from badlands of a later age in northwestern New Mexico comes a parade of giant dinosaurs: duckbilled *Kritosaurus*

and *Parasaurolophus*, horned *Pentaceratops*, *Albertosaurus*—a 30-foot relative of the legendary *Tyrannosaurus rex*—and *Alamosaurus*, a long-necked beast with a "whiplash" tail. (Though this plant-eater also lived in Texas, the "Alamo" in its name comes from a spring by that name just south of Farmington, New Mexico.) In short, badlands can be bountiful.

Painted Desert Badlands in Petrified Forest National Park (below) erode quickly, exposing a treasure-trove of fossils. Petrified logs tumble into gullies as they emerge from ancient deposits of volcanic ash (right). Pronghorn "antelope" are among the many living creatures that populate the park today (bottom left).

Water Is

"A river does not just happen; it
has a beginning and an end. Its
story is written in rich earth, in
ice, and in water-carved stone,
and its story as the lifeblood of
the land is filled with colour,
music, and thunder."

ANDY RUSSELL

WHERE there's water, there's life.

In arid lands, plants and animals flourish in the narrow, well-vegetated strips along streambanks. Though small, these riverbank communities—known as **riparian habitats**—are essential to the survival of most desert animal life. In Arizona, more than 60% of the state's wildlife species depend on the 1% of the land that is riparian. In the Southwest, such habitats are easy to spot from any high vantage point. Lined with trees—cottonwood, sycamore, ash, and willow—watercourses show up as green ribbons woven through the surrounding desert landscape.

The Virgin River flows through Zion National Park (left). A mule deer near the Fremont River within Capitol Reef National Park (above).

LIFEBLOOD OF THE SOUTHWEST

This map shows the region's 15 dams over 250 feet (76 m) in height. Not shown are another 270 dams 100-249 feet (30 m-76 m) tall within the same area.

Water, more than anything else, has shaped the course of human history in arid lands. When water vanishes, civilizations unravel. On the Colorado Plateau, ancient Pueblo people are thought to have left their cliff houses in the 13th century during a period of prolonged drought. And later, about 200-300 years before Europeans arrived, the Hohokam of southern Arizona vacated their communities. These prehistoric farmers had engineered a sophisticated system of irrigation canals but were evidently unable to cope with catastrophic floods and droughts that struck between A.D. 1358 and 1385.

WATER, WATER, EVERYWHERE?

Artificial lakes, pools, and fountains pacify residents and visitors to the arid Southwest. Roosevelt Lake is an odd sight in the Sonoran Desert (opposite, bottom); and Colorado River water that's pumped into lakes, pools, and fountains to dress up Las Vegas mirrors the city's extravagant light show generated by Colorado River water at Hoover Dam.

Today, our burgeoning cities share a thirst for water that's on the reckless side. Phoenix and Tucson alone now represent more than 3.4 million human desert dwellers, with their estimated water use (in Phoenix) at 300+ gallons *per person per day.* In Tucson, which has relied on groundwater for drinking, reserves have dropped by more than 200 feet (61 m) in the past 50 years.

Some locals say that on a quiet desert night, if you listen carefully, you might hear a muffled sucking sound. That sound is said to come from the Central Arizona Project, an open-air aqueduct built to help Arizonans suck water from the overstressed Colorado River, whose water is now being shared by seven western states and Mexico. The Colorado was once a river mighty enough to let steamboats ply upstream from the Gulf of California. Now, entering the Colorado from the Gulf is best done in a shallow-draft boat like a canoe or kayak, if it's possible at all.

As a species, we pride ourselves in being able to analyze and plot our destiny. How well are we doing?

OVERLEAF ▶

A dizzying view of Glen Canyon and the Colorado River below the dam, at Horseshoe Bend Overlook.

Arizona has more registered boats per capita than any other state in the union—about 2.3 boats/100 residents in 1998.

The Army Corps of Engineers reports that, nationwide, the most common primary purpose for which dams are built is recreation—35%. In desert areas, dam builders say that water storage and flood control are the main benefits. Hydroelectric power accounts for only 2% of the intended use for our nation's dams.

Equally surprising, about 56% of the electricity in the United States is generated by burning coal, and the lion's share of the rest comes from burning oil and natural gas.

Millions flock to Lake Powell for outdoor recreation each year. Lilly Langlie from Norway (below) enjoys a campfire after a long day of boating on the lake. Natural dams created by lava flows in the Grand Canyon (opposite, top)—once blocked the Colorado River. Photograph by Ken Hamblin

MOVING MOUNTAINS

Shortly before Glen Canyon Dam was completed in 1964, the Colorado River carried nearly half-a-million tons of sediment and rocky debris through the Grand Canyon every day. Put another way, large (five-ton) dump trucks filled with this same debris would be speeding by at a rate of one per second.

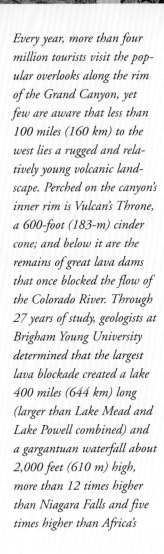

LAVA DAMS ALONG THE COLORADO

Every year, more than four million tourists visit the popular overlooks along the rim of the Grand Canyon, yet few are aware that less than 100 miles (160 km) to the west lies a rugged and relatively young volcanic landscape. Perched on the canyon's inner rim is Vulcan's Throne, a 600-foot (183-m) cinder cone; and below it are the remains of great lava dams that once blocked the flow of the Colorado River. Through 27 years of study, geologists at Brigham Young University determined that the largest lava blockade created a lake 400 miles (644 km) long (larger than Lake Mead and Lake Powell combined) and a gargantuan waterfall about 2,000 feet (610 m) high, more than 12 times higher than Niagara Falls and five times higher than Africa's Victoria Falls. But erosion and the accumulation of silt behind the dam destroyed it in just a few thousand years. Completed in 1964, Glen Canyon Dam is only one of 16 major dams and 50 smaller dams engineered to detain and divert water from the Colorado River and its tributaries. None of the dams is a permanent feature of the landscape—no dam is. Scientists predict that Lake Powell will be full of mud within 700-800 years, and it's unlikely that any of these dams will last that long.

Canyons

THE GRAND CANYON is a place of awesome proportions, defying simple description. The Hualapai Indians, who live on the canyon's south rim, tell of a great flood that once covered the Earth, and that to drain away the flood, a mythical hero beat the ground with a knife and club, creating the canyon's chasm. On seeing the Grand Canyon for the first time, most visitors suppose that the Colorado River must once have been far larger than it is today, perhaps as wide as the canyon itself.

At Toroweap, on the Grand Canyon's north rim, a brave soul can walk to the edge and look straight down for 3,000 feet (914 m) to the Colorado River below. How did this great gorge, a mile deep and roughly 11 miles (18 km) wide, come to be?

Water and gravity are the main forces that have carved the Grand Canyon. As the Colorado Plateau rose to its present elevation (see Face of the Land), the Colorado River began slicing into its cracked and faulted surface. The young river wore away a narrow strip scarcely wider than itself. Over the past 10 million years, right up to the present, the canyon has been widening by the countless tributaries and gullies that form on its sides. Cliff walls gradually crumble and fall, accelerated by freezing and thawing—when water freezes in crevices, it expands, forcing rocks apart. As heavy rains wash this rocky debris into the river, it is then carried downstream.

Words and photographs can't prepare you for that first look into Arizona's Grand Canyon—nothing can. More than 6,000 feet (1,829 m) deep in places, 277 miles (446 km) long, and up to 18 miles (29 km) across, the vast, brilliantly hued, stair-step landscape is, for most visitors, Nature's most spectacular creation. Because this is dry country, few plants hide the canyon's raw magnificence.

But even greater than the rugged expanse of buttes and promontories, "temples" and "thrones," is the sense of time captured in the mile-thick stack of layered rock. Rocks at the rim were laid down about 250 million years ago, just before the Age of Dinosaurs, and remnants of ancient bedrock exposed at the bottom of the gorge are nearly two billion years old, a time when only the simplest forms of life existed on Earth (see Stories in Stone).

Down-cutting in the Grand Canyon peaked during the last Ice Age, the Pleistocene, when the climate was wetter and colder than today. Floods from violent summer storms and melting ice in the Rockies were even more dramatic and powerful then, but the same forces are at work today. The Canyon's rims are farther apart than underlying layers simply because rocks at the top have been exposed to erosion the longest.

Measured from Crystal Ridge on the North Rim to the bottom of Grand Canyon in the Middle Granite Gorge section of the river, the Grand is 6,720 feet (2,048 m) deep, making it the third deepest canyon in North America. The deepest canyon lies along the Oregon-Idaho border in a remote corner of the West, where the Snake River carved the volcanic walls of Hells

Canyon to a depth of nearly 8,000 feet (2,438 m). Contrary to popular belief, the deepest canyon in Mexico is not one of the magnificent gorges in the Copper Canyon complex; it's the No de Piaxtla in the state of Durango, estimated to be 7,500 feet (2,286 m) deep, making this the second deepest canyon in North America.

Canyon Shapes

THE SHAPES OF CANYONS and gorges are defined by the types of bedrock in which they form. When rivers cut into harder rocks like granite, gneiss, or well-cemented sandstone, the results are straight-walled, U-shaped canyons such as Utah's Zion Canyon and Arizona's Canyon de Chelly. In softer bedrock—siltstone or shale, for example—rivers carve V-shaped, more gently sloping sides, similar to the gullies that prevail in badlands. In the Grand Canyon and many other canyons on the Colorado Plateau, erosion of alternating layers of harder and softer bedrock creates a stair-step effect. The harder rock layers erode into cliffs, and soft layers into slopes, forming, in the case of the Grand Canyon, one of the finest stair-step canyons in the world.

SHAPELY CANYONS

An aerial view of Canyon de Chelly (this page, top), clearly shows its sheer-walled "U" shape . Grand Canyon, viewed from the North Rim (opposite, top) is a classic stair-step canyon . Badlands (right), seen here from Zabriskie Point, Death Valley, features "V" shaped gullies carved in soft, fine-grained sediments—deposits from a lake that once filled the valley. Immediately above, another "V" shaped canyon, a cut chiseled by the Rio Diablo tributary of the Little Colorado River in northern Arizona.

CURVACEOUS CANYONS

At Goosenecks State Park (shown here), near Mexican Hat, Utah, only narrow "necks" of land separate tight bends in the San Juan River as it meanders in graceful loops, almost doubling back upon itself. Equally spectacular are the panoramic views of great bends in the Colorado River from overlooks at Dead Horse Point State Park (near the Island in the Sky district of Canyonlands National Park) and at Horseshoe Bend in Glen Canyon, a few miles south of the dam. (See pages 120-121.)

Springs, Ciénegas, + Travertine

A RELIABLE WATER SOURCE is a rare find in the Southwest's otherwise thirsty landscape. Not surprisingly, most Native Americans and European settlers laid claim to river valleys and places fed by natural springs.

Even in the arid Southwest, permanent springs or streams can create small marshy wetlands, locally known as **ciénegas** (Spanish for *cien aguas,* meaning *hundred waters*) or **pantanos** (swamps). Mastodons drank from them, prehistoric Indians lived close to them, and Spanish and English-speaking peoples tapped them for agriculture and ranching. Once a prominent feature of arid landscapes in southern New Mexico and Arizona, ciénegas took a severe beating during the historical era of overgrazing in the late 19th century. Today, only 15 of these natural marshlands remain in Arizona and New Mexico combined.

Arivaca Ciénega (above)—part of the Buenos Aires National Wildlife Refuge in southern Arizona—is one of the few natural, spring-fed marshlands to have survived in the Southwest.

Quitobaquito Spring (left) is a small, natural oasis in the Sonoran Desert that's home to a unique pupfish, shown life-size below. Illustration by David Fischer.

OASES

Tucked away in mountain canyons of southern California, western Arizona, and northern Baja California are oases of native desert fan palms. These palms are a sure sign of mild winters and a constant source of water. In California's Coachella Valley, where groundwater follows fractures to the surface along the San Andreas Fault, palm oases are numerous and aligned with the fault. Among the best places to visit the 70 or so palm oases in the Southwest are California's Andreas Canyon and Palm Canyon near Palm Springs, Borrego Palm Canyon in Anza-Borrego State Park, five places within Joshua Tree National Park, and Arizona's Palm Canyon in the Kofa National Wildlife Refuge.

Some oases occur in what seem to be improbable places—flat, otherwise dry, desert scrub at the edge of a mountain range. These, too, form along fault lines, where the shifting earth has blocked the normal flow of underground water and forced it to the surface. Two noteworthy examples are Quitobaquito Spring on the Mexican-American border in Organ Pipe Cactus National Monument and Ash Meadows National Wildlife Refuge in southern Nevada not far from Death Valley. Thirty springs that surface in Ash Meadows allow life to flourish here. For its size—22,117 acres—this refuge hosts the highest number of endemic species (26) anywhere in the United States. Intermingled with its long and varied history of human occupation, Quitobaquito is an oasis for more than 270 species of plants, no less than 100 species of birds, and a unique pupfish.

Some of the Southwest's natural waterways have been preserved by their isolation. For about 700 years, in a remote canyon, the Havasupai—*people of the blue-green water*—have made their home beside an unusual creek that drains into the Grand Canyon. This is a place of mysterious beauty, a wonderland of mineral dams and draperies, enchanting pools, waterfalls, and hanging gardens that nourish body and soul. The mineralized fantasies and surreal aquamarine blue color of Havasu Creek come from the stream's limy water. Whatever it touches it coats with a milky encrustation called **travertine**—calcium carbonate, or calcite—that hardens on contact with air. Travertine drips from streamside cliffs like frozen waterfalls and builds elaborate terraces over tree roots and floating accumulations of debris. Windblown spray encases plants and will speckle your spectacles. Water saturated with calcium carbonate reflects more blue-green than other wavelengths of light, giving the creek its dazzling color.

Havasu Creek starts as rainwater on the plateau above. The plateau's porous limestone and sandstone layers, which dip towards Havasu Canyon, allow water to seep downward, picking up minerals along the way. Deeper down, the water meets an impenetrable layer of rock and begins to flow sideways, eventually emerging into the light of day on the canyon floor. From such modest beginnings, it's hard to imagine that, at full strength, this little stream flows at 38 million gallons per day.

Aerial view of Havasu Canyon (above), showing Mooney Falls in the foreground and Havasu Falls at the top, where the canyon splits. The village of Supai lies two miles farther upstream. A devastating flood that ripped through Havasu Canyon in 1990—the canyon's worst flood since 1935—destroyed most of the travertine dams (left) in lower reaches of the canyon and completely changed the appearance of Havasu Falls (right—the way it looked just four months before the flood). No human lives were lost, but the flood wrecked havoc with Supai, killed horses and pets, and uprooted hundreds of trees.

Weird and wonderful mineral formations line the shores and poke up from the depths of California's Mono Lake. These **tufa** (*TOO-fah*) towers (above) form exclusively underwater, but today visitors can see these exotic formations because the lake has been dramatically reduced by diversions begun in 1941 to supply the city of Los Angeles with water.

Farther south, more than 500 tufa towers can be seen in the dry bed of ancient Lake Searles on the edge of the Mojave Desert. Known as the Trona Pinnacles, these towers—some as tall as 140 feet (43 m)—formed about 20,000 years ago when the climate was wetter and water filled the lake. Tufa towers are made when calcium-rich waters from underground springs mix with lake water that is rich in carbonates. The resulting mineral, calcium carbonate (calcite), is a more porous form of travertine. Living creatures often use calcium carbonate for housing projects: humans make cement from it, and aquatic animals build coral reefs and shells from it.

BIRDING BONANZAS

Water birds abound in the arid Southwest. Our sparse, shallow, often salty lakes are natural fueling stations for millions of migrating and resident birds. In the absence of fish, these alkaline lakes teem with fairy shrimp, brine flies, and other invertebrate foods. Also scattered throughout the Southwest are marshy wetlands fed by freshwater springs and streams, prime nesting habitat for numerous water birds. Many wildlife "hot spots" that have survived 20th century human expansion are now protected as National Wildlife Refuges or preserves held by The Nature Conservancy. Mono Lake and Willcox Playa are important exceptions. To find these wetlands, check the website listings i the rear of this book.

The biggest inland lake in California—the Salton "Sea"— is also the weirdest in the West. It looks out of place, smells out of place, and in fact is the result of an accident. Nearly a century ago, an agricultural dike broke and flooded an enormous ancient dry lake basin with Colorado River water. Situated in a hot desert valley of southern California, the Salton Sea has no outflow and its only inflow is chemical-laced runoff from nearby farmlands. It is now 25% saltier than sea water. The lake is rich with introduced fish, a boon for migrating birds and fishermen; but periodic die-offs from pollution and rising salinity have killed as many as 8 million fish in one day. While the future of the Salton Sea is uncertain, wetlands in the desert Southwest are growing so scarce that the lake is worth reviving, if possible. Recent studies show that the Salton Sea attracts more species of migrating birds than any other location in the lower 48 states, except for the Texas coast. Winter is the best time to visit.

Shallow, salty desert lakes—Mono Lake, for example (opposite, top; bottom)—teem with fairy shrimp, brine flies, and other critters that nourish millions of migrating birds, including the American avocet (opposite, center). Photo by Gary Kramer

Hanging Gardens

IN DEEP DESERT CANYONS on the Colorado Plateau, it's not uncommon to find cool places where water seeps from the sandstone walls. Sandstone is often quite porous, up to 20% air, allowing rainwater to soak into the plateau above and travel downward. If it meets a harder layer of rock, the water will flow sideways, where it may emerge on a cliff face as a dripping spring. Such springs support luxuriant hanging gardens of ferns, columbines, monkeyflowers, and shooting stars. Among the most famous are those visible along the trails in Zion National Park that lead to Weeping Rock, the Emerald Pools, and the Virgin River Narrows.

Spring-fed drips and wispy waterfalls nourish hanging gardens in Zion National Park (left and right). The wet canyon walls are festooned with columbine, shooting star, and maidenhair fern (below, left to right).

Surfaces

"The light is psychedelic, the dry electric air narcotic. To me the desert . . . sharpens and heightens vision, touch, hearing, taste, and smell. Each stone, each plant, each grain of sand exists in and for itself with a clarity that is undimmed by any suggestion of a different realm."

EDWARD ABBEY

DESERT strips away the non-essentials. In endless, unobstructed views, "The desert reveals itself nakedly and cruelly, with no meaning but its own existence," says Edward Abbey in *Desert Solitaire*.

No plow has furrowed it; no fence confines it. The sense of untouched terrain prevails. Human presence is so slight you might wonder whether you are the first to witness it. The rocks call you to trace the slipface of an ancient dune frozen in time, to feel rough, crusty lichen bodies. They invite you to run your fingers over the rippled surface of a ropy lava flow and along the faithful contours of a tree turned to agate.

Colorful badlands spread below Arizona's Vermilion Cliffs (left); Above, an ocotillo in Anza-Borrego Desert State Park.

Harsh environments weed-out distractions, allowing our senses to focus on each living entity, individually and as part of an organized whole. Plants growing in brutally hot lava and cinder fields of Mexico's Pinacate Mountains (above) seem to reflect the order of a Japanese garden.

An unfolding bud of strawberry hedgehog cactus (left); barrel cactus flowers (lower right); and a collared lizard lounging on a hot rock (bottom left) emblazon spots of living color on southwestern landscapes.

gravel, a bird call pierces the silence. Sounds, colors, and textures seep into the soul.

Hot surfaces blaze, an artist's palette of crimson, ocher, burnt sienna, and magenta against the fierce blue above. As clouds race by, patches of landscape soften—vibrant colors fade to pastels. As the sun nears the horizon, colors intensify. Lengthening shadows throw landforms into sharp relief and unmask hidden textures. At sunset, rock colors bleed into the sky, then quickly fade to silhouettes against the Milky Way.

With darkness, temperature plummets. You build a campfire, just as the Old Ones did—to warm your hands, to cook, and to pay respect to spirits that wander this wild and enchanted land.

In gentler places beyond the desert realm, plants clothe surfaces in green and soften harsh outlines. But here the plants are more like exclamation marks. Strange shapes and spines speak of their struggle. Rain releases the scents of pungent creosotebush, musky desert willow, and sweet mesquite. Often as unpredictable as they are astounding, tapestries of wildflowers ornament the land, filling the air with perfumes of lupine, sand verbena, or evening primrose. Cactus flowers shout their presence—in scarlet, shocking pink, cadmium orange, and canary yellow. The desert blossoms with abandon, then reverts to quiet waiting.

We step from a modern life of busy clutter to a primeval state of simple sensation. Sounds are magnified in the clear air. A lizard skitters faintly, deer give themselves away with a swish of

Colors: Science + Symbolism

In Southwestern curio shops you're bound to find decorative sand paintings framed and ready to hang as wall art. But to the Navajo, **sandpainting** is much more than a commercial enterprise. It's part of a curing ritual that's practiced today just as it was hundreds of years ago. The designs are sacred and have been handed down for generations from one singer to another. The singer—usually a man—and his assistants use colored sands, minerals, and finely ground charcoal for the pattern, sometimes adding crushed flowers, leaves, pollen, or cornmeal. With the exception of red, which symbolizes protective forces, the primary sandpainting colors represent the cardinal directions. In general, black is *north;* white, *east;* yellow, *west;* and blue, *south.* Dry pigment is sprinkled from between thumb and forefinger onto a smoothed bed of neutral sand or onto a buckskin spread on the ground. Like the sand artists of Tibet,

Among hand prints in Canyon de Chelly National Monument rests a painted Kokopeli (right, top), known to many as the "hump-backed flute player." He has appeared in the Southwest for at least 800 years, on rock surfaces from Chihuahua, Mexico, to the Colorado Plateau and west into California. Legends say he embodies purity, joy, fertility, or the coming of spring. In Mystery Valley (right, bottom), someone seems to have marked time on a sandstone wall beneath a "running man" pictograph.

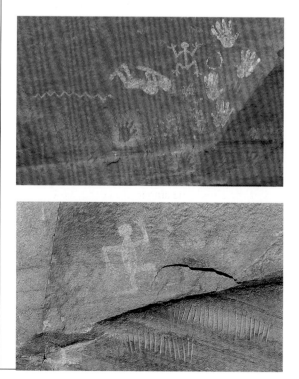

Navajo painters work from the center toward the edges so that they don't disturb the pattern. An error can be covered with the background sand and overpainted with the correct lines.

At some point during the ceremony—typically held at night in the company of friends and relatives—the patient sits on the completed sandpainting to gain power from the gods represented in the design. The healer also rubs the patient with pigments from the painting to absorb evil responsible for the illness. The work must be created and destroyed within one day, and, at the end of the ritual, the singer places the sand beneath a bush or tree to return the medium to the elements.

Other, less ephemeral types of Native American art decorate the Southwest. Pictographs are images painted on rock surfaces by applying pigments—white from gypsum, red from iron-rich minerals, and black from charcoal. Pine gum or the juice of yucca plants often served as glue to make the paint stick. Pictographs are plentiful in the Grand Canyon, Canyon de Chelly, and the Sedona area of Arizona; in eastern Utah, especially in and north of Canyonlands National Park; and in western Texas at Hueco Tanks State Historical Park.

Canyon de Chelly National Monument is loaded with rock art, including several story panels of Navajo origin. Within the mix of prehistoric and historic pictographs above, the mounted riders with spears presumably depict Spaniards who arrived in the canyon during the 17th century.

Most rock art in the Southwest was not painted—it was made by chipping through natural patinas that coat rock surfaces (left). Prehistoric Pueblo people created the bighorn sheep above in Monument Valley and the petroglyph panel below in Canyon de Chelly National Monument.

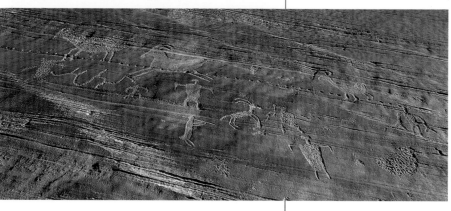

In Nature's desert art gallery, early Americans also inscribed images on sun-baked boulders and sandstone cliffs coated with **rock varnish** (often called **"desert" varnish**, though it's not limited to deserts). These natural patinas come in hues of red-brown, blue-gray, or black, determined by the amount of manganese oxide (black) and iron oxide (red) present. Recent studies suggest that colonies of bacteria living on exposed surfaces can capture trace minerals and dust from the atmosphere and deposit them as a thin veneer of oxides. This build-up, which includes clay, takes thousands of years to mature. Using stone tools, Native American artists could easily chip through varnish patinas to reveal lighter, uncoated rock beneath. As a form emerged—perhaps a bighorn sheep or an antelope—a **petroglyph** was created.

Some of the most intriguing and best preserved rock art in the world is found in the American Southwest. Commonly represented are human shapes, animals, tools, clothing, weather phenomena, the sun, moon, stars, plants, supernatural entities, and mythical creatures. Their exact meanings as intended by the artist will never be known. A bighorn sheep, for example, might have been more than an animal drawing— it could have been the depiction of a mythical clan ancestor.

Called Tse Hane, "rock that tells a story," by the Navajo, Newspaper Rock (below) is one of the best examples of a rock art panel in the Southwest. About 2,000 years of graphic story-telling are recorded here as petroglyphs, from prehistoric through historic times.

IN LIVING COLOR

The yellow, orange, blue, gray, green, and black splotches that coat rocks in the most inhospitable areas of the world are primitive creatures, lichens. Lichens are colonies of two separate entities working together: an alga lives within the framework of filaments built by a fungus and uses photosynthesis to nourish itself and its host. Because the colony may grow no more than a few millimeters per century, it may be thousands of years old.

Fragile yet tenacious pioneers, lichens are among the first to colonize a barren rocky surface. If their environment dries out, they lose up to 98% of their water and remain dormant. When rain or dew returns, they swell and come back to life. Lichens affect their host rock physically and chemically, etching its surface, but their main source of mineral nutrients comes from airborne dust. By helping to make and hold soil, lichens open the way for higher plants to gain a foothold.

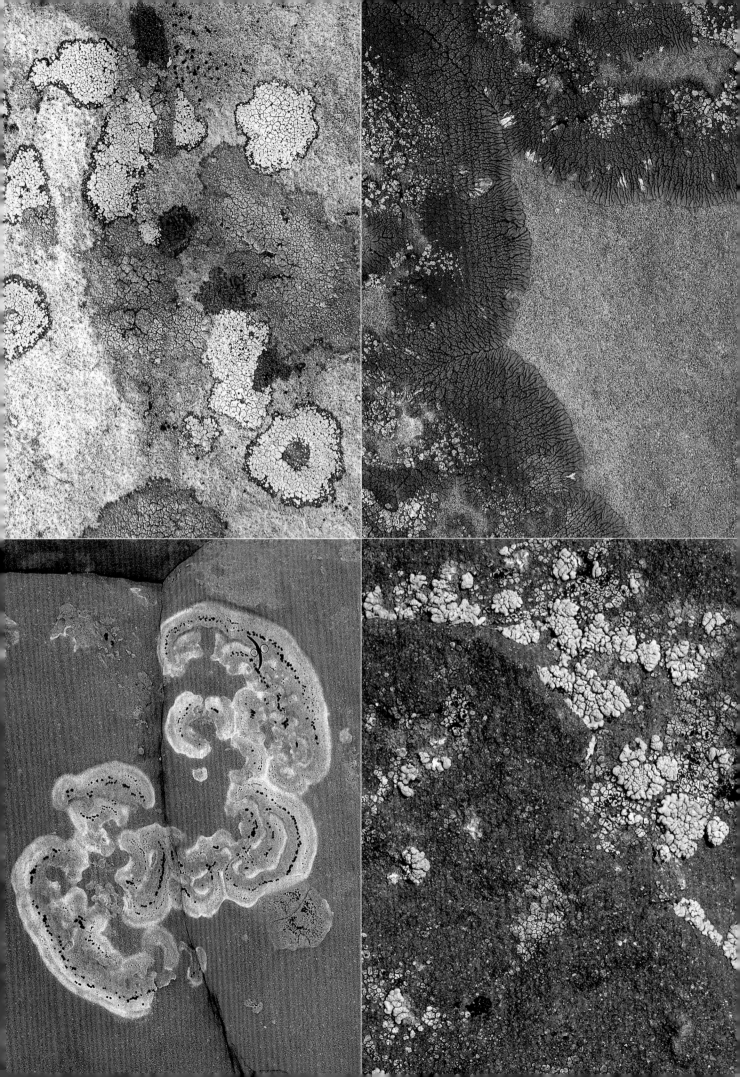

Nature's Paint-Pot

IRON MINUS OXYGEN

Greenish, light blue, and off-white colors in badlands scenery of Petrified Forest National Park came from iron deposited in places without oxygen. Concentrations of this *reduced* iron formed in prehistoric marshes and under stagnant water. An outcrop of siltstone rich in reduced iron (left) can be seen by the parking lot at the trailhead to Delicate Arch in Arches National Park.

GYPSUM

The snow-white dunes at White Sands National Monument, New Mexico, are entirely composed of gypsum. Alabaster, selenite, and satin spar are varieties of the same mineral. Gypsum is the main ingredient in plaster and drywall (sheet-rock) used in house construction.

H E M A T I T E   (I R O N   P L U S   O X Y G E N)

Hematite (red ocher), more commonly
known as rust or iron oxide, is
responsible for the reds, red-browns,
and purples seen in many places on the
Colorado Plateau. Hematite deposits
indicate a hot, dry climate when the
rock was formed, in the presence of
oxygen.

L I M O N I T E

Limonite (yellow and brown ocher) is a general term
for brown iron oxide bonded with water (also called
goethite). Limonite adds tints of yellow and orange
to the petrified sand dunes on the east side of Zion
National Park.

Dune sand comes in all colors, determined
by its parent rock. Most dunes consist of
quartz stained various shades of red or
orange by iron: dunes take on golden
hues in Death Valley and in Great Sand
Dunes National Monument, and hues of
rosy pink in southern Utah.

D U N E   S A N D

FROM NATURE'S PAINT POT

COPPER

A tiny pinch of copper will turn white rocks bright green or azure blue. Turquoise, malachite, azurite, and chrysocolla are all copper-bearing gemstones. Native Americans used azurite for face-painting and pottery-tinting more than a millennium ago, and it was the most important blue pigment used by European artists during the Renaissance. The finer the grind, the lighter the blue. Coarsely ground, premium grade azurite is richly colored but difficult to mix into a water-based painting medium. As oil painting increased in popularity, fewer aritsts used azurite—in oil the pigment loses its ability to reflect blue light and turns black.

QUARTZ

The Great White Throne, a prominent sandstone landmark in Zion National Park, owes its whiteness to a relatively pure deposit of quartz sand in its upper layers.

Volcanic rocks rich in quartz and feldspar are light in color. Two of them, andesite and rhyolite, come in shades ranging from medium gray and buff to lavender and pink.

MICA

In Death Valley, the green hues seen at Artists Palette come from mica decomposing into clay.

URANIUM

A smidgen of uranium transforms rocks to canary yellow or yellowish-green.

CARBON

Black and dark gray sedimentary rocks contain incompletely decomposed plant and animal matter (carbon) that was preserved in stagnant swamps. The black colors of coal and oil are also due to carbon.

MAGNESIUM

The high content of magnesium and iron in basalt lava imparts a black or dark gray color to this volcanic rock.

MANGANESE

A touch of manganese supplies the purple hues at Artists Palette in Death Valley. And manganese added to glass in bottles made before World War I causes them to turn purple when exposed to sunlight.

MALACHITE

CHRYSOCOLLA

MILK QUARTZ

AZURITE

TURQUOISE

MICA

COAL

MAGNESIUM

MANGANÉSE

URANIUM

SUN-STRUCK
MANGANESE GLASS

To vanish before the eyes of a predator, an animal's body outline can be as important as color and pattern. Uneven, broken edges make a shape more difficult to detect; and most horned lizards come equipped with fringing scales, an enhancement in body armor that helps to complete the disguise.

Those unfortunate enough to be seen and captured by a bird, snake, or mammal have a few other tricks that come into play. Sharp spines that decorate the head of some species can get caught in a predator's throat, and blood that's sometimes squirted from the eyes is foul-tasting to coyotes, foxes, and kin.

Two short-horned lizards, the same species (*Phrynosoma douglassi*) in different habitats (above). One lives on the rocky floor of a pine forest just outside of Cedar Breaks National Monument (top) and the other frequents chalky limestone deposits along the edge of the Bryce amphitheater (bottom).

Born to Blend In

As you explore desert and canyon country of the Southwest, sooner or later, out of the corner of your eye you'll detect a rock on the move. You pause to study the earthly tapestry at your feet while trying to figure out what went where, but all's still, as rocks should be. Then, just as you've decided that your imagination must be working overtime, something moves again, this time clearly caught in the act. Frozen among the rocks sits a creature perfectly matched in color and form—short, fat, and flat—a "horny toad" for sure. Although somewhat toad-like in shape, these animals are actually lizards. But unlike most lizards, their short legs and stubby tails aren't designed for quick dashes to safety.

Horned lizards are widespread in the West, and all seven species are masters of disguise. Although they cannot perform chameleon-like feats of color change, these docile lizards are born with pre-determined colors and patterns that match the soil and rocks where they live. Even within a single species, you'll see red animals among red rocks and yellow animals on yellowish ones. Dark splotches resemble shadows, and colorful flecks can resemble lichens. Predators are quick to spot those that don't blend-in—a classic example of survival of the fittest. Individuals that best match the background are those most likely to live, reproduce, and pass on their genes to future generations.

Where found in south Texas, the Texas horned lizard (*Phrynosoma cornutum*) is perfectly matched to reddish sand (left). And two regal horned lizards (*Phrynosoma solare*) vanish into their rocky surroundings in the Tucson Mountains (above and in oval).

Textures + Patterns Underfoot

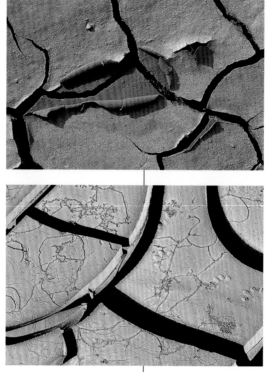

GEOMETRIC SHAPES IN THE MUD— we've all seen them in gardens and along the edges of ponds and rivers. But in arid lands, where cycles of wetting and drying are the norm, patterned ground is often a striking feature of the landscape. And every pattern has a story to tell.

Suppose you find a dry lakebed with thin curls of mud peeling from the surface; and the mud is broken into a pattern of nearly perfect six-sided geometric shapes with wide cracks between them. The curls say that the mud was covered with fresh water—when salty mud dries, the edges along cracks don't curl upward, they bend downward. The symmetrical honeycomb pattern says that the mud dried uniformly. When mud dries unevenly, the cracks grow in curved rather than in straight lines, making polygons with irregular sides, often four to seven. And the relatively wide cracks suggest that the mud is mostly clay. Mud with more sand than clay doesn't shrink as much as it dries and produces a coarser pattern of shapes with narrower cracks between them.

An experienced mud detective would also know whether the lake had dried slowly or quickly. Lakebeds that take a long time to dry crack deeply and form large geometric patterns. Some of the giant polygons in ancient southwestern lakebeds are each about the size of a football field, so large that the patterns can only be seen from the air; and the cracks between them are 3-4 feet wide and up to 50 feet (15 m) deep. The longer the mud takes to dry, the deeper the cracks. Evidently, these playa lakes dried very slowly, probably over a period of years. The cracks are now filled with silt or sand. These features have been spotted in Death Valley National Park, in the North Panamint Valley Playa.

In much of Death Valley, salt pans have formed where ancient lakes evaporated. As salt crusts dry out, they fracture into polygonal patterns like those seen in drying mud. But, unlike mud, where moisture persists and seeps up through the cracks, these salt polygons will grow as salt crystals form around the edges. Under just the right conditions, neighboring plates will meet, keep growing, push against each other, and form salt saucers with upturned edges. When flooding rains arrive, such features dissolve away, to regrow as the playa dries out.

The shattered bases of telephone poles on the Bonneville Salt Flats attest to the destructive power of salt crystals. When rains come, dissolving the surface salt on the old lakebed, the saline water creeps up into the pole. As it dries out, salt crystals grow within pores of the wood. Eventually the foot of the pole shatters.

Compare the two photographs on this page. Both show irregular geometric shapes in the mud with upturned edges, telling us that the mud was once covered with fresh water and that the surface dried unevenly. But in one—the bottom photograph—the cracks are wider, deeper, and smoother. This says that the mud contains more clay and dried more slowly than the sample above it.

In Death Valley, salty mud flats (left) dry and crack into geometric shapes without upturned edges. And in the dune fields (bottom), rain washes wind-gathered dust into hollows, forming mud puddles. As the mud shrinks, sand settles into the cracks. Below: Desert pavement of petrified wood chips in Arizona's Petrified Forest National Park.

DESERT PAVEMENT

Surfaces that appear purposely fitted with a tight mosaic of pebbles and cobbles are a common sight in the desert. The origins of desert pavement have long puzzled geologists, and studies suggest that the process varies from place to place. In some areas, wind blows away the silt and sand-sized particles, leaving the heavier gravels behind. In other places, repeated cycles of wetting and drying are the cause. When wet, the soil expands and the rocks are lifted. When dry, the soil cracks as it shrinks, and fine-grained particles settle into the gaps.

The naked smoothness of eroded sandstone commonly referred to as **slickrock** can be found throughout most of the Colorado Plateau. The name probably originated with the early pioneers who found almost any kind of solid rock to be slick to their iron-rimmed wagon wheels and their iron-shod horses. Today's rubber tires and shoes provide better traction, and only when dusted with sand or snow does slickrock really live up to its name.

When you enter arid landscapes of the Southwest, especially on the Colorado Plateau, watch out for more than rattlesnakes. Those knobby black soil-crusts you might be stepping on are mature, living communities of helpful micro-organisms (above). These colonies enrich the soil with nitrogen and help prevent erosion. The black crust is called **cryptobiotic** (Greek for *hidden life*) soil, and the most prominent organism in these tiny communities is one of the oldest life forms on Earth, cyanobacteria. As the bacteria grow and move through the ground, they leave behind a sticky glue, forming an intricate web of fibers that hold soil particles together. And when wet, these fibers store water—they can swell up to 10 times their dry size with water, a benefit to the colony and other organisms as well. Unfortunately, the fibers that give strength to these crusts are easily crushed by cattle, vehicles, and foot traffic. What took decades to build can be quickly destroyed. So watch where you walk— stay in the washes, on established trails, or on bare expanses of rock.

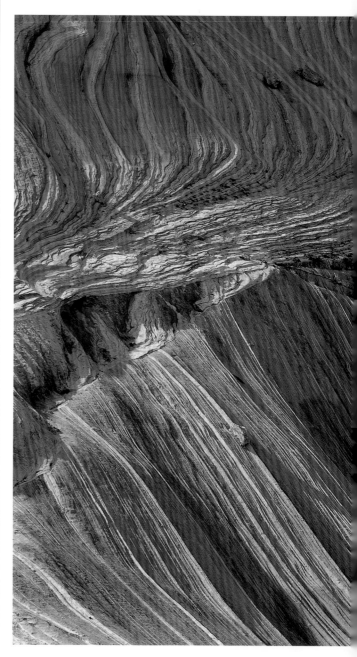

Caution! Watch out for living crusts of cryptobiotic soil (far left), common to many sandy landscapes of the Colorado Plateau. Below, slickrock terrain in the Paria Canyon-Vermilion Cliffs Wilderness.

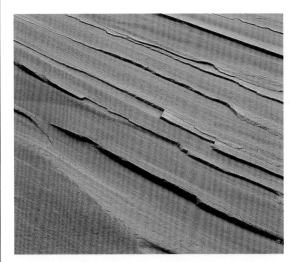

Artfully Weathered Walls

As cliffs freeze and thaw, heat and cool, vast slabs of sandstone break away, here adding sculptural relief to the sheer walls of Spearhead Mesa in Monument Valley (below).

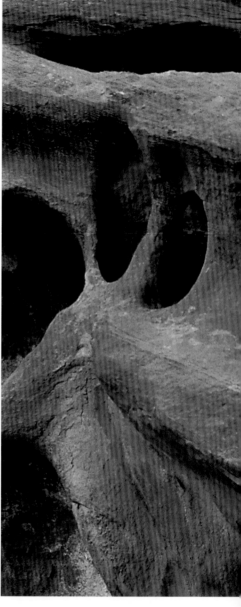

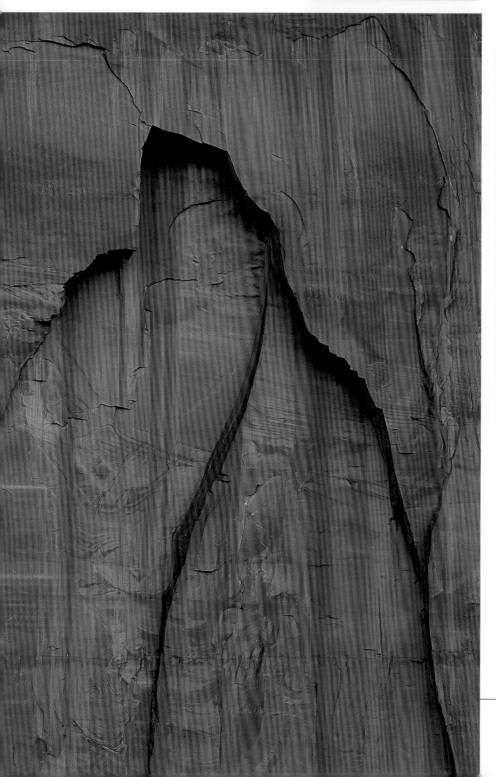

Rock walls in canyon country weather in uneven ways. Surfaces most exposed to the elements will wear away the fastest. Weak spots fracture, opening cavities for decay. The variables seem as mysterious as they are endless, and it's no wonder that even geologists remain puzzled by the complexities.

As you travel through canyon country, look for weathered cliff faces or cavities (also known as tafoni) under overhangs. You'll discover an intricately sculpted world of miniature arches, tiny honeycombed passages, and fluted columns—an abstract realm sure to catch the eye of the photographer.

Mystery Valley (above, both images) and Capitol Reef National Park (right) are two places among thousands in the Southwest where surfaces weather into fantasies of form.

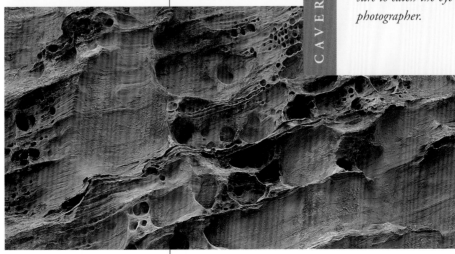

Stories

"It is not the strongest of the species that survive, nor the most intelligent, but the one most responsive to change."

CHARLES DARWIN

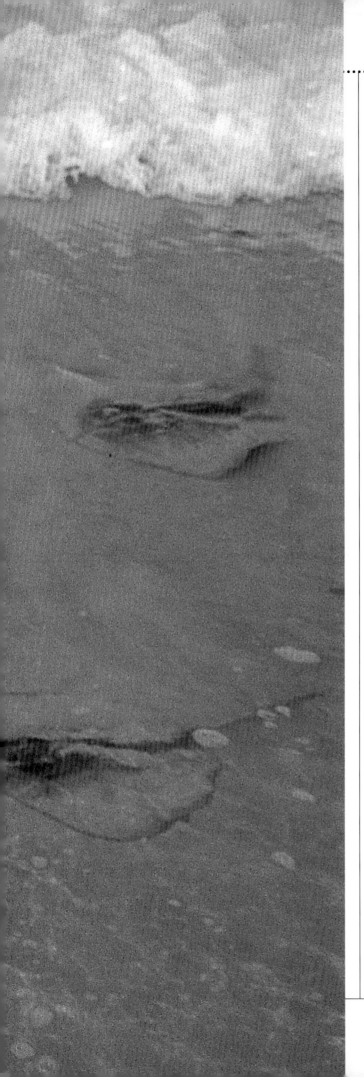

"I'VE GOT SOME oceanfront property in Arizona ..." sang George Strait in his 1986 number-one hit tune "Oceanfront Property." Though said in jest, these words ring true, if you turn back the clock far enough. For millions of years, Arizona, like much of the Southwest, was swimming with stingrays and sharks, and we don't mean Corvettes and card sharks. Entombed here in ancient layers of rock are fossilized sea creatures, and among them are rays and sharks of the fishy kind.

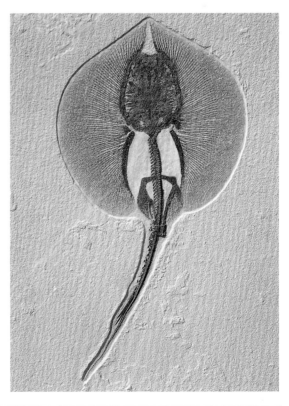

Stingrays in the Galápagos Islands (left), modern relatives of those that once lived in the American West (above).

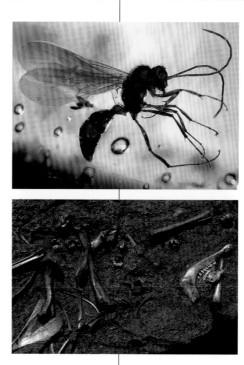

Fossils (from Latin, for *something dug up*) are the remains of ancient animals and plants—usually a hard part, such as a tooth, shell, or tree trunk—preserved in rock. When buried, the hard parts may be replaced by minerals carried in groundwater or may dissolve away, leaving merely an impression. Sometimes, only a trace of an animal's behavior is left behind, such as a burrow, track, or coprolite (fossilized feces). Occasionally, a complete animal is preserved, such as a mosquito encased in amber (fossil tree resin), or a saber-tooth cat trapped in tar. Freezing and mummification are rare forms of fossilization. Among the more spectacular finds are Ice Age mammoths frozen in the Siberian tundra and desiccated remains of ground sloths that died some 13,000 years ago in southwestern caves.

By definition, fossils are old—prehistoric organisms preserved thousands, millions, even billions of years in the past. Nearly 200 years ago, **paleontologists** (Greek for *scientists who study ancient beings*) discovered that fossils occur in an orderly sequence. Older fossils were in the lower sedimentary layers, the first to be deposited, and the younger fossils were on top, in the more recent deposits. Knowing this allowed geoscientists to determine the **relative ages** of fossil-bearing rocks (older vs. younger), which quickly led to the development of a worldwide **geologic time scale**, a calendar showing the history of life on Earth (see pp. 164-165). Later dating techniques, such as measuring the rate of decay of radioactive elements, have allowed geologists to assign **absolute ages** to nearby rocks (usually volcanic) that don't contain fossils. At archaeological sites and very recent deposits containing trees or freshwater clamshells, scientists could also measure time by counting yearly growth rings.

The calendar of life in rock is divided into four major **eras**—Precambrian, Paleozoic, Mesozoic, and Cenozoic—the last three of which are separated by catastrophic extinctions of life on Earth. Eras are further subdivided into **periods**, and the periods into **epochs** (see pp. 164-165). But in exploring the Southwest, you'll see and hear many other names in a geologist's vocabulary—the Kaibab Formation, the Barstow Formation, and the Kayenta Formation, for example. To understand and map the earth history of an area, geologists identify and name rock **formations**. A formation is a body of rock with characteristics that distinguish it from all neighboring rocks. Most formations have been named after a geographic feature (such as the Kaibab Plateau) or a place (Barstow, California; Kayenta, Arizona). The Pierre Shale, a formation extensively seen throughout the West and named after the capital of South Dakota, contains fossil shark teeth and marine reptiles from the time when dinosaurs ruled the land.

FOSSILS IN MANY FORMS

A wasp sealed in amber (fossilized sap that oozed from a tree in the Dominican Republic about 40 million years ago) and the bones of an elk trapped in a California tar pit 10-40 thousand years ago (above, stacked) help bring the past to life. Once filled with mud, the shell of this snail (below, left) dissolved away, leaving only a stone cast (called a *steinkern*) of its corkscrew-shaped interior.

FOSSILIZED FOOTPRINTS

Animals leave tracks behind when they cross soft ground, such as a mud flat or a layer of volcanic ash. If these impressions remain undisturbed, and are quickly covered by another layer of sediment to protect them, they are sometimes preserved when the sediment hardens into rock.

Many museums feature rock slabs with fossilized footprints, but travelers who want to see dinosaur tracks in the wild can find information about no less than a dozen sites in the West through the websites given at the back of this book.

MORE UNUSUAL FOSSILS

Most leaves are relatively fragile and decompose quickly, but they occasionally turn up as fossils with stunning detail. This sycamore leaf (left), for example, settled into a muddy Utah lake bottom about 46 million years ago. Even an animal's tracks can be fossilized. The big track (above) left in an area just west of today's Tuba City, Arizona, belonged to *Dilophosaurus,* a 20-foot-long (6-m) flesh-eating dinosaur (right).

Dinosaur sculpture by John Fischner

LIFE ON EARTH: A CHRONOLOGY

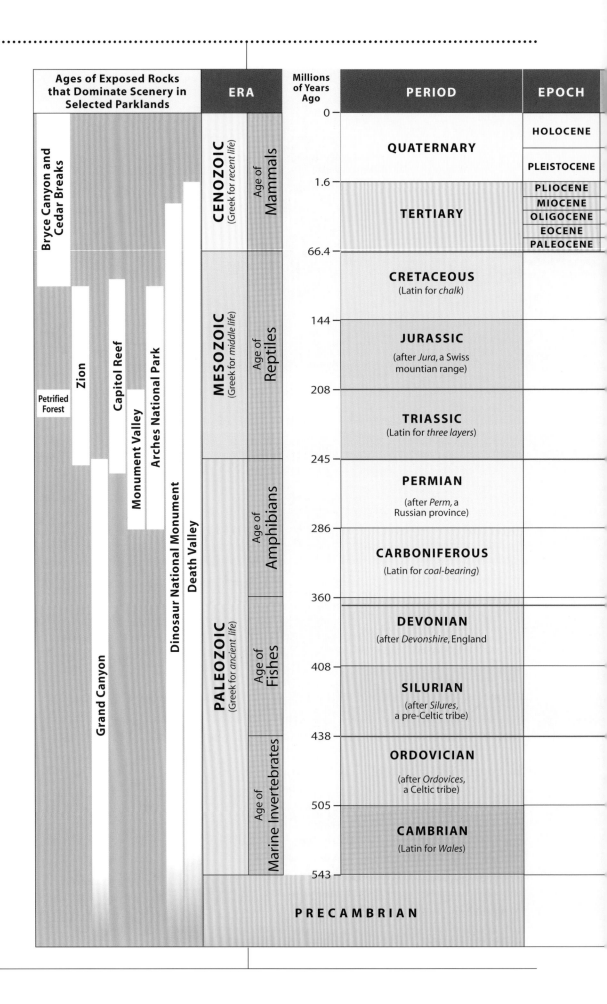

Ages of Exposed Rocks that Dominate Scenery in Selected Parklands	ERA		Millions of Years Ago	PERIOD	EPOCH
Bryce Canyon and Cedar Breaks	CENOZOIC (Greek for recent life)	Age of Mammals	0	QUATERNARY	HOLOCENE
					PLEISTOCENE
			1.6	TERTIARY	PLIOCENE
					MIOCENE
					OLIGOCENE
					EOCENE
					PALEOCENE
Petrified Forest / Zion / Capitol Reef / Monument Valley / Arches National Park	MESOZOIC (Greek for middle life)	Age of Reptiles	66.4	CRETACEOUS (Latin for chalk)	
			144	JURASSIC (after Jura, a Swiss mountian range)	
			208	TRIASSIC (Latin for three layers)	
Grand Canyon / Dinosaur National Monument / Death Valley	PALEOZOIC (Greek for ancient life)	Age of Amphibians	245	PERMIAN (after Perm, a Russian province)	
			286	CARBONIFEROUS (Latin for coal-bearing)	
		Age of Fishes	360	DEVONIAN (after Devonshire, England	
			408	SILURIAN (after Silures, a pre-Celtic tribe)	
		Age of Marine Invertebrates	438	ORDOVICIAN (after Ordovices, a Celtic tribe)	
			505	CAMBRIAN (Latin for Wales)	
			543	PRECAMBRIAN	

History of Life

(Greek for *complete*) Present to 10,000 years ago;
Modern life forms

(Greek for *most recent*) Last Ice Age ends 10,000 years ago; first *Homo sapiens* & cave paintings;
time of giant land mammals: mammoths, mastodons, ground sloths, camels,   saber-toothed cats

(Greek for *more recent*) First Australopithecines, Neanderthals, & toolmaking

(Greek for *less recent*) First signs of early man, whales

(Greek for *brief*) First anthropoid apes & grasses

(Greek for *dawn*) First large land & sea mammals

(Greek for *ancient*) Explosive rise of land mammals

66.4 million years ago: Famous K-T (Cretaceous-Tertiary) Mass Extinction. All dinosaurs and 75% of all species suddenly vanished: likely cause, an asteroid collides with Earth.

Dinosaurs rule the land & air.
First primates, snakes, & flowering plants.
In the sea, ammonites and giant reptiles abound;
first mosasaurs.

Dinosaurs flourishing.
First squids, frogs, salamanders, birds, & placental mammals
Early mammals mostly small and nocturnal.

208 million years ago: mass extinction; about 75% of all species lost.

First crocodiles, turtles, lizards, & small dinosaurs.
Coniferous trees & cycads abound

245 million years ago: mass extinction, the largest ever; about 95% of all species lost.

Abundant amphibians, some giants.
Mammal-like reptiles dominate land.
Rise of large trees: ferns, conifers, ginkgos, & cycads

Numerous amphibians and first reptiles.
First spiders & flying insects.
Great coal-forming forests of ferns, club mosses, & horsetails .

367 million years ago: mass extinction; about 80% of all species lost.

First land vertebrates (amphibians).
Scale trees, rushes, horsetails, & ferns evolving on land.
Sharks, armored fish, ammonites, & sea scorpions colonize the ocean.

First evidence of animals on land: centipedes and other arthropods
(animals with jointed external skeletons).
Land plants appear.

438 million years ago: mass extinction; about 85% of all aquatic species lost.

First corals, sea stars, & freshwater fish.

Proliferation of marine animals with hard external skeletons, including molluscs, brachiopods, & trilobites.
First animals with backbones (vertebrates): jawless fish.
Some unusual soft-bodied forms preserved in shale.

Few fossils. First simple forms of life: bacteria, aquatic algae, & jellyfish.
Earliest signs of life: single-celled organisms without nuclei–about 3.5 billion years old.

Earth's crust begins to form: about 4.55 billion years. ago

Missing Fossils, Missing Layers, Missing Time

EACH FOSSIL is a minor miracle. Right from the start, the odds were against it. For a plant or animal to become a fossil, it must be buried quickly. If not, the remains may be destroyed by scavengers or decay. Even after being "safely" buried, if its chemical environment proves unfavorable or the temperature is too high, the hard parts may dissolve or melt. Earth movements or the sheer weight of overlying sediments may crush the organism beyond recognition. If a fossil remains intact to emerge once again at the surface, chances are good that weathering and erosion will destroy it before paleontologists can find and collect it.

The record of Earth history is not complete. There are gaps in the rock record that geoscientists call **unconformities**. These gaps represent extensive periods of erosion, times when sediments were being stripped away faster than they were being deposited. One cycle of uplift and erosion long ago could have erased rock layers that represented an entire era of Earth history!

Sometimes, rock layers exposed in one area are missing from nearby areas. In New Mexico, for instance, Jurassic dinosaurs are found only in the northern half of the state. *Stegosaurus, Allosaurus,* and *Camarasaurus* are the most common species, but *Seismosaurus,* one of the world's longest dinosaurs—about 130 feet (40 m) head-to-tail— is there, too. Yet, in the southern part of New Mexico, dinosaurs from this period are missing. Why? Perhaps rocks of Jurassic age have eroded away; perhaps they were never deposited there in the first place; or maybe they have been covered or destroyed by volcanic activity.

Considering the geological events that have shaped and re-shaped the face of our planet over incomprehensible periods of time, fossils are nothing short of miraculous. Imagine the odds against finding the nearly perfect impression of a delicate moth that died in Colorado 34 million years ago (above). Photo by Amanda Cook/Florissant Fossil Beds National Monument.

Fossilized remains of two dinosaurs that roamed much of the West—*Stegosaurus* (left) and *Camarasaurus* (below)—are often not found where you would expect them to be. Their bones or rocks that could contain them turn up missing from the fossil record. Our picture of the past can never be **complete.** Sculptures by John Fischner

A *Camarasaurus* skull (above), on exhibit in the dinosaur quarry at Dinosaur National Monument. Sculptural reconstruction of head (far left) by John Fischner

Two other creatures from the past: an ammonite (left), an extinct relative of octopuses and squids; and *Priscacara*, a perch-sized fish that lived in the lakes of northern Utah and Colorado and south-western Wyoming 45 million years ago.

Ancient Landscapes

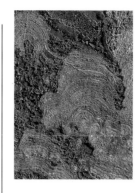

IN MOUNTAINS flanking Death Valley and a few other places in the Southwest, paleontologists have discovered the first signs of life in our region— fossilized mats of blue-green algae (stromatolites) and tunnels made by worm-like creatures. These primitive life forms are preserved here in rocks that date back to the **Precambrian era**, which ended 543 million years ago.

During the **Paleozoic** (*ancient life*) **era**, which lasted for 298 million years, life exploded in the oceans and crept onto the continents. Sea animals developed shells or armor-like skeletons, which greatly increased their chances of being preserved as fossils.

Shallow Paleozoic seas repeatedly covered and retreated from the Southwest. Locally, there were shallow tropical reefs, lagoons, and islands akin to what we see today in the Bahamas or the

Columns of cyanobacteria—stromatolites (above)— more than 2 billion years old, are probably the first signs of life on Earth visible to the naked eye. Horsetails (left) are today's knee-high, streamside relatives of some that grew as trees in the Paleozoic era. *Dimetrodon* (below) is one of the pelycosaurs, mammal-like reptiles that ruled the land shortly before the Age of Dinosaurs. Its sail may have been used for heat regulation and social display. Sculpture by John Fischner. In the circular inset is a fossilized *Dimetrodon* track found in southern New Mexico.

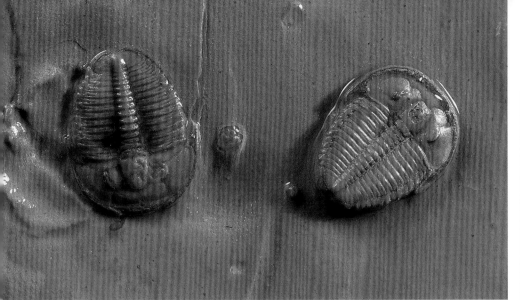

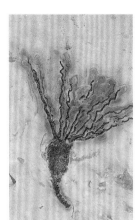

Mississippi Delta. These seas were home to early fishes, including sharks, as well as countless invertebrate animals: corals, trilobites, crinoids (relatives of starfish), bryozoans, brachiopods, and assorted mollusks (clams and extinct kin to octopuses and squids). Plant life expanded onto a continent divided by huge slow-moving rivers. Toward the end of this era, land animals flourished. In marshes of ferns, horsetails, and club mosses lived giant amphibians—six feet of sluggishness with huge, toothy, spade-shaped heads and long tails. Insects, reptiles, and coniferous trees spread across the land. Pelycosaurs, mammal-like reptiles with a spiny sail along the back, lived among scorpions and, yes, cockroaches.

Shallow seas once covered much of the West. Trilobites (top left)—extinct relatives of insects, crabs, and spiders—scuttled around on the sea floor and were tremendously successful early in the Paleozoic era. The feather star (top right)—a free-floating crinoid related to starfish—used its feathery arms to comb the water for food particles; a few descendants of crinoids live today. Both fossils pictured above were found in Utah. An elegant, 320-million-year-old disc fish (left), a small species about the size of the palm of your hand, was unearthed in Montana.

Then came the **Age of Reptiles**, the **Mesozoic** (or *middle life*) era, which spanned about 180 million years. Although 95% of all shallow-marine species mysteriously vanished at the end of the Paleozoic, mollusks quickly filled their places. Many land-dwellers survived the mass extinction, including those that gave rise to birds, mammals, and flowering plants. Also among the survivors were reptiles, which as a group, achieved unparalleled prominence at this time. Vast river floodplains, coastal swamps, and tropical forests became home to fearsome crocodile-like predators, the phytosaurs, some reaching lengths of 30 feet (9 m). And dinosaurs, though small at first, quickly populated the land. Halfway through the Mesozoic, during the Jurassic period, giant dinosaurs ruled. Much of the West was populated by duckbilled, horned, and carnivorous forms. In the sea were huge turtles and long-necked, paddling plesiosaurs. Flying reptiles soared overhead, while lizards and small mammals scurried underfoot. But reptilian glory days came to an abrupt end approximately 66 million years ago, marking the close of the Cretaceous period (see page 51).

Forests of tree ferns, cycads (left), and conifers flourished during the Age of Reptiles. Among them were the great *Araucarioxylon* trees now turned to stone in Arizona's Petrified Forest National Park. National Park Service photo

An animated swarm of stemless crinoids (below) was preserved in shale deposits of late Mesozoic age from Colorado.

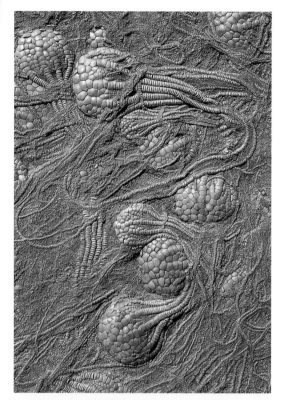

Dinosaurs ruled the West during much of the Age of Reptiles. *Chasmosaurus* (opposite, bottom), a cousin of *Triceratops*, possibly used its giant bony frill for social display and as a shield. Its sharp beak was well suited to shearing plant foods. *Chasmosaurus* bones have been found in both Canada and New Mexico. *Ceratosaurus* (left), a scaled-down version of *Allosaurus*, was a well-equipped predator that stood about the height of humans today. Its domain included parts of Utah and Colorado, as well as East Africa. Dinosaur sculptures by John Fischner.

Stygimoloch (right), the *thorny devil*, is one of the bone-headed dinosaurs, a group of plant-eaters with extremely thick skulls and little room for a brain in their soccer-ball sized heads. The dense skull, at least in some species, probably offered protection in head-butting contests, similar to tests of strength seen today between male bighorn sheep. Ammonites (below) flourished for more than 300 million years. Their extinction coincided with catastrophic events that also wiped out the dinosaurs. This fossil turned up in Texas.

The demise of dinosaurs ushered in the **Age of Mammals**, the **Cenozoic** (or *modern life*) **era**, which covers the last 66 million years of Earth's history. New species of mammals and birds evolved rapidly in the absence of dinosaurs. Flora and fauna flourished in and around subtropical lakes and streams. The Green River Formation, one of the richest fossil deposits in the world, contains palm fronds, tropical flowers, dragonflies, turtles, crocodiles, and more than 25 varieties of fish. Away from the water lived primitive browsers, early carnivores, primates, insectivores, and rodents. Condylarths, the size of house cats, were among the most important early mammals. They gave rise to all hoofed mammals, elephantine forms, whales, and dolphins. New to the Southwest were small primates akin to lemurs, hippopotamus-like animals, flightless birds that stood seven feet tall, and, of particular importance, grasses.

As savanna-like grasslands expanded, so did the numbers and types of grazing animals, including camels, rhinoceroses, long-horned bison, three-toed horses, mastodons, and mammoths. Wolves, lions, and short-faced bears fed on the herbivores. Humans entered North America at the very end of this era, arriving in the Southwest at least 11,000 years ago. Soon after, camels, horses, saber-tooth cats, and all of the giant mammals became extinct. Was there a connection? Perhaps. The timing fits closely, and archaeologists have found spear points among the bones at mammoth and mastodon kill sites. But the relative importance of human hunters in the downfall of these creatures remains a mystery.

Riches of the Utah-Colorado-Wyoming Green River Formation: a palm frond (left); a common herring-like fish, *Gosiutichthys* (above); and a snapping turtle (far right).

Sometimes called the saber-toothed tiger, *Smilodon*—a lion-sized giant among saber-tooth cats—probably stalked prehistoric horses, antelope, and deer in grasslands and open woodlands of the Southwest. Most likely, this unusual cat went for the throat of its prey with these 7-inch (18-cm) dagger-like canine teeth (below).

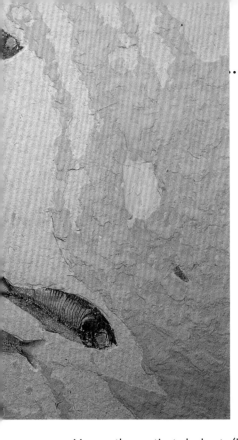

Mammoths—extinct elephants (below)—once populated most continents of the world; and as humans were evolving, so too were mammoths. Early *Homo sapiens* hunted them in the Southwest and elsewhere, some say to the point of extinction, but the debate goes on.

ARIZONA

Petrified wood of a giant conifer, *Araucarioxylon arizonicum.* In honor of Petrified Forest National Park, this tree was named the official state fossil in 1988. In Paiute mythology, petrified logs were the scattered remains of broken spears from a fierce battle among the gods. Today, we know that living trees coexisted with dinosaurs; many fell and were buried in swampy bottomlands, eventually entombed in layers of ash and clay. Over a long period of time, water containing silica and other dissolved minerals penetrated the wood and crystallized within the cells, turning the logs to stone.

CALIFORNIA

A sabertooth cat, *Smilodon fatalis.* Bones of nearly 2,000 of these lion-sized cats have been recovered from the world-renowned Rancho La Brea tar pits in Los Angeles. *Smilodon* lived in the Southwest during the last Ice Age and disappeared about 11,000 years ago, about the same time that humans first populated the region. Unlike any modern cat, this predator could open its mouth so wide that it could stab prey with its enormous dagger-like canine teeth.

Designating fossils as official state emblems didn't begin until 1967, and some states have yet to follow suit. Dinosaurs lead the pack for popularity, and they rule the West; where found in the East, they have been honored as well. New Jersey's official state fossil is a duckbill dinosaur, and two other states—Connecticut and Massachusetts—chose dinosaur tracks as their state fossils. Here's our summary for the Southwest.

OFFICIAL STATE FOSSILS

COLORADO

A plant-eating dinosaur with a double row of large plates down the neck and back, *Stegosaurus stenops. Stegosaurus* is well represented in finds at Dinosaur National Monument, where a life-sized model is on display. Adults reached 30 feet (9 m) in length and weighed about two tons.

NEVADA

A streamlined, somewhat dolphin-like, sea-going reptile, an ichthyosaur, *Shonisaurus popularis.* This "fishy lizard" was not a dinosaur, but lived during the Age of Dinosaurs and was big, up to 50 feet (15 m) long. Nevada's Berlin-Ichthyosaur State Park contains the best preserved ichthyosaurs in North

America. The site features the remains of 37 of these reptiles that might have become stranded together in a shallow lagoon some 225 million years ago.

NEW MEXICO

The oldest and tiniest (10-foot) state dinosaur, *Coelophysis,* one of the first dinosaurs on Earth (of Triassic age) and one of the best known. It was a long-necked, long-tailed, small-headed meat-eater that ran on its hind legs. Hundreds of skeletons were unearthed during the 1940s at Ghost Ranch (near Abiquiu), home of artist Georgia O'Keeffe and site of the Ruth Hall Museum of Paleontology.

TEXAS

A colossal thick-bodied dinosaur, *Pleurocoelus,* a long-necked plant-eater related to the better-known *Brachiosaurus.* At 30-50 feet (9-15 m) long, it's the biggest state fossil—as befits Texas. In some respects, its tracks—found from Del Rio to Dallas and beyond—are more famous than the animal's skeletal remains. Some of its fossilized saucer-like footprints are over three feet in length, and groupings indicate that these dinosaurs traveled in herds. You can see them in Dinosaur Valley State Park near Glen Rose in central Texas.

UTAH

Allosaurus fragilis, a big-headed, bipedal, flesh-eating dinosaur akin to *T. rex.* Believe it or not, no state has yet staked a claim to *Tyrannosaurus* for its state fossil. Though not quite so famous, *Allosaurus* was equally ferocious, with teeth as long as bananas, housed in a body as long as a bus. The Cleveland-Lloyd Dinosaur Quarry, a National Natural Landmark 30 miles (48 km) south of Price, Utah, is the world's main source of *Allosaurus* skeletons and is open to visitors.

Illustrations by Paul Mirocha and David Fischer

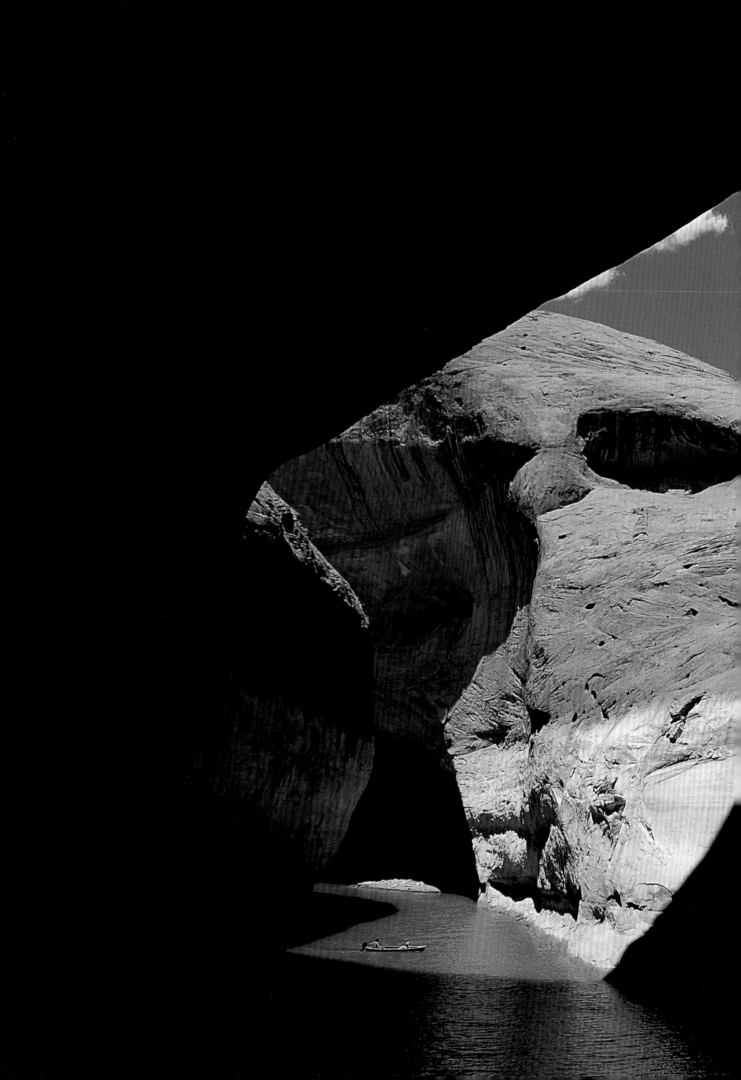

Where to Find Them

An Annotated List of Southwestern Parks and other Notable Sites of Geological Interest

KEY TO SYMBOLS

L LODGING IN OR WITHIN 10 MILES OF PARK ENTRY POINTS

C ESTABLISHED CAMPING AREAS WITHIN PARK, ACCESSIBLE BY CAR; ONLY SOME HAVE MOTOR HOME HOOK-UPS—CONTACT PARK FOR DETAILS

F FOOD IN PARK OR WITHIN 10 MILES OF ENTRY POINTS (INCLUDES CAMPING SUPPLY STORES, SNACK BARS, AND/OR RESTAURANTS)

R RESTROOMS OR PIT TOILETS AVAILABLE IN PARK

W WATER AVAILABLE IN PARK, BUT NOTE THAT MANY PARKS IN THE WEST ARE HUGE AND OFFER WATER IN FEW PLACES, SO CARRY A GOOD SUPPLY WITH YOU, AT LEAST ONE GALLON PER PERSON PER DAY

B BACKCOUNTRY HIKING AND BACKPACKING OPTIONS AVAILABLE; PERMITS ARE REQUIRED IN MOST PARKS

P AN EXTREMELY PRIMITIVE AREA; COME FULLY PREPARED TO BE SELF-SUFFICIENT

NOTE: IN MANY PARKS, PETS ARE NOT ALLOWED ON TRAILS; CALL AHEAD OR CONSULT WEBSITES FOR REGULATIONS

ABBREVIATIONS

SR = STATE ROAD

US = US HIGHWAY

I = INTERSTATE HIGHWAY

RD = ROAD

MI = MILE/MILES

FT = FOOT/FEET

TTY = TELEPHONE SERVICES FOR THE DEAF AND HEARING IMPAIRED

BLM = BUREAU OF LAND MANAGEMENT

R = RIVER

What Is a National Monument?

"A national monument is intended to preserve at least one nationally significant resource. It is usually smaller than a national park and lacks its diversity of attractions."

In the region covered by this book, eight new national monuments were designated between January 2000 and January 2001, and all have been added to this 2004 updated edition.

Anza-Borrego Desert State Park, CA.

ACOMA PUEBLO

P.O. Box 309, Acomita, NM 87034.
Tel: 505-552-6604;
http://puebloofacoma.org/

West of Albuquerque lies the ancient pueblo of the Acoma perched high atop a sandstone **mesa** bordered by sheer cliffs. It commands a breathtaking view of other mesas, valleys, and distant mountains—no wonder it's called Sky City. Native guides are available on-site to take you up to the village, one of the longest-occupied sites in North America. No photography permitted. FRW

AGUA FRIA NATIONAL MONUMENT

Established Jan. 2000. BLM Phoenix Field Office, 21605 N. 7th Ave., Phoenix, AZ 85027. Tel: 623-580-5500;
http://www.az.blm.gov/aguafria/
pmesa.htm or http://arizona.sierraclub.
org/monuments

A high semi-desert grassland **plateau** dissected by the steep Agua Fria River **canyon** with pristine riparian forest. Two **mesas**—Perry Mesa and Black Mesa—shelter a complex of late **prehistoric sites**, among the largest in the Southwest; all are remote. This rugged, somewhat isolated monument is ideal for hiking, primitive camping, and wildlife watching; no facilities. Follow "Leave No Trace" guidelines. No collecting! Only 40 mi N of Phoenix: take I-17 to Bloody Basin Rd (Exit 259)—head E to cross the monument (4-wheel, high-clearance vehicle recommended); or at Exit 256, take Badger Springs Rd (dirt but suitable for all vehicles) E to a boulder area—follow trail SE to river (a mile hike; feet may get wet). No off-roading. LFBP (lodging in Cordes Lakes, Black Canyon City, and Meyer)

ANTELOPE CANYON

For information, contact the John Wesley Powell Memorial Museum & Visitor Center, P.O. Box 547, Page, AZ 86040. Tel: 928-645-9496 or 888-597-6873; http://www.americansouthwest.net/ slot_canyons

Perhaps the most stunning and accessible **slot canyon** in the world. Located on Navajo land near Page, AZ, marked by signs along SR-98 just west of the Navajo Generating Station (Milepost 299). A phantasmagoria of sandstone swirls and changing light. Tour guides available for hire through the John Wesley Powell Museum or often on-site; access fees are charged. The upper section of the canyon is flat; the lower section (0.5 mi farther E along SR-98) is outfitted with several sturdy step-ladders (see Slot Canyons Can Be Deadly, p. 104). LCFP

ANTELOPE ISLAND STATE PARK

(see Great Salt Lake)

ANZA-BORREGO DESERT STATE PARK

200 Palm Canyon Dr., Borrego Springs, CA 92004. Tel: 760-767-5311; http://www.anzaborrego.statepark.org/

Visit the largest desert state park in the contiguous USA with over 600,000 acres—wildflowers, cacti, hidden **palm canyons**, a **hot spring**, and wildlife galore. In the park's vast **badlands**, over 500 different types of fossils, including mammoths, have been discovered. Anza-Borrego encompasses 500 mi of dirt roads and 110 mi of riding and hiking trails. Located on the eastern side of San Diego County about 2 hours from San Diego, Riverside, and Palm Springs. LCFP

ARCHES NATIONAL PARK

P.O. Box 907, Moab, UT 84532. Tel: 435-719-2299 (voice), 719-2319 (TTY); http://www.nps.gov/arch

Rio Grande gorge, Santa Elena Canyon, Big Bend National Park. Photo by William Dupré.

More than 2,000 **arches** and **windows** of every size and shape—the greatest density of natural arches in the world. Also showcased in the park are massive sandstone **fins, pinnacles, balanced rocks,** and other extraordinary shapes. Many formations can be seen from the park road. Short foot trails lead to some of the arches; others require a more extensive hike. The park is loaded with fragile **cryptobiotic soil,** so kindly watch your step. LCFRW(seasonal)B

BANDELIER NATIONAL MONUMENT

HCR1, Box 1, Suite 15, Los Alamos, NM 87544. Tel: 505-672-3861; http://www.nps.gov/band/

An unexpected delight nestled in the heart of the Jemez Mtns., an area formed by repeated **volcanic activity**. Here ancient history blends with geological wonders. **Cliff dwellings** are nestled in the Bandelier Tuff, formed by two explosive eruptions from Valles **Caldera** 1.0 and 1.5 million years ago; each explosion was 600 times more powerful than that of Mt. St. Helens. Wind and rain have eroded the soft tuff into unusual tent-shaped **pinnacles,** not well developed in this park (for the best examples, visit Kasha-Katuwe Tent Rocks National Monument). Follow the Falls Trail for a view of the **Rio Grande Rift** and a fascinating walk into a **maar crater.** LCFRWB

BIG BEND NATIONAL PARK

P.O. Box 129, Big Bend National Park, TX 79834. Tel: 915-477-2251; http://www.nps.gov/bibe/

The abundance, diversity, and complexity of rock formations make this park a geological paradise. Here on the eastern margin of the **Basin and Range** region, down-dropped basins and uplifted mountains and three deep **canyons** carved by the Rio Grande form the core of Big Bend. The park sits in the Chihuahuan Desert and has been designated a World Biosphere Reserve in recognition of its unique plant and animal life. Hiking and river trips are the best ways to appreciate all that the park has to offer. LCFRWP

BISTI/ DE-NA-ZIN WILDERNESS AREA

BLM, Farmington Field Area Office, 1235 La Plata Highway, Farmington, NM 87401. Tel: 505-599-8900

A newly created wilderness that encompasses 45,000 acres of incredibly rugged, arid **badlands** about 30 mi S of Farmington. For back-country explorers only. Take SR-371 from Farmington S. After 37 mi, turn left on gravel road; it's 2 mi to trailhead. Two miles along the entrance drive, the grassy plain is replaced by the multi-colored badlands. Exercise care—you'll find unstable surfaces and fragile formations. P

BLACK CANYON OF THE GUNNISON NATIONAL PARK, CURECANTI NATIONAL RECREATION AREA

102 Elk Creek, Gunnison, CO 81230. Tel: 970-641-2337; http://www.nps.gov/blca/

No other canyon in North America combines the narrow opening, precipitous walls, and awesome depths of Black Canyon. The "black" refers to the canyon's shadowy depths and the hard, dark rock (mostly gneiss, schist, and granite) that forms its craggy walls. Roads along both north and south rims take you to the canyon's very edge. The drives are not connected. The more accessible South Rim is 15 mi E of Montrose, via US-50 and SR-347, offers many scenic overlooks and trails. LCFRW, seasonal

BLACK ROCK DESERT PLAYA

BLM Winnemucca Field Office, 5100 E. Winnemucca Blvd., Winnemucca, NV 89445. Tel: 775-623-1500; http://www.nv.blm.gov/Winnemucca/recreation/Black_Rock_Desert.htm

Located just north of the small town of Gerlach in NW Nevada. People come from hundreds of miles to test cars, launch rockets, fly hot-air balloons, and sail across these wide-open flats—one of America's largest playas, which stretches for 25 mi. Its name comes from a prominent volcanic and sedimentary outcrop that rises from the lake bed. This seasonally flooded basin is usually dry from June to September; but before driving on the cracked, silty surface, stop and check for soft mud. Take a chance, and you will get stuck. It's also the site of a small photogenic **geyser** (Fly Geyser) on private land that formed during a drilling operation. LFP

BONNEVILLE SALT FLATS

BLM, Salt Lake District, 2370 South 2300 West, Salt Lake City, Utah 84119. Tel: 801-977-4300; http://www.utah.com/places/public_lands/bonneville_salt.htm/

A portion of Utah's largest playa—the Great Salt Lake Desert—one remnant of ancient Lake Bonneville, a vast Ice Age lake that was ten times larger than the Great Salt Lake of today. The Bonneville Salt Flats is the flattest part of the playa, with ideal conditions for auto racing. But beware: summer thunderstorms and winter rains can turn the playa to impassable mud. There are no facilities or services available on the salt flats. Camping is restricted to surrounding public lands and private facilities in Wendover. P

BOSQUE DEL APACHE NATIONAL WILDLIFE REFUGE

P. O. Box 1246, Socorro, NM 87801. Tel: 505-835-1828; http://southwest.fws.gov/refuges/newmex/bosque.html

A hotspot for wildlife viewing and photography, one of the richest wetlands in the West. This oasis is situated in the floodplain of the Rio Grande on the northern edge of the Chihuahuan Desert. Every autumn, tens of thousands of migrating birds—including cranes, Arctic geese, hawks, eagles, and many kinds of ducks—gather in the refuge for the winter. Seasonal hunting and fishing is permitted in designated areas. The refuge is located about 20 mi S of Socorro. From I-25 S, take Exit 139, head E on US-380 for less than 0.5 mi, and then go S on SR-1 for 8 mi to refuge; from I-25 N, use Exit 124, take SR-128 E for 1 mi, then N on SR-1 for 11 mi to Visitor Center. LC(for educational groups only with reservations)FRW

BOULDER DAM (see Lake Mead National Recreation Area)

BRYCE CANYON NATIONAL PARK

P.O. Box 170001, Bryce Canyon, UT 84717. Tel: 435-834-5322; http://www.nps.gov/brca/

A must-see—**hoodooland** itself! Castles and spires and mazes of colorful, eroded sediments. Not a canyon in the strict sense; the hoodoos stand in a natural amphitheater along the weathered edge of the Paunsaugunt **Plateau.** Tour the many scenic overlooks along the rim road or follow any of the breathtaking trails within the canyon. Open year-round, but most trails are closed by winter snow and ice. LCFRW

CABEZA PRIETA NATIONAL WILDLIFE REFUGE

1611 N. 2nd Ave., Ajo AZ 85321. Tel: 520-387-6483; http://www.publiclands.org/html or http://southwest.fws.gov/refuges/arizona/cabeza.html

An exceptionally remote Sonoran Desert landscape bordering Organ Pipe Cactus National Monument to the north and west. This is a place of rugged **mountains, bajadas,** and broad valleys dotted with **sand dunes** and **malpais.** Cabeza Prieta, Spanish for *dark head,* refers to a lava-topped granite peak within the refuge. Home to a great diversity of wildlife, including rare and endangered species—bighorn sheep, Sonoran pronghorn, lesser long-nosed bats, pygmy owls, desert tortoises, among others. Many animals depend upon **tinajas** for water here. Rough roads—4-wheel drive vehicles are required on all routes except one. No facilities. Entry permit required—this airspace is in use for tactical training and visitors must sign a Military Hold Harmless Agreement. For a permit, contact the refuge office in Ajo. The eastern two-thirds of the refuge is closed from March 15 to July 15 every year, the fawning season for Sonoran pronghorn. LF (in Ajo) BP

CANELO HILLS CIÉNEGA RESERVE

P.O. Box 815, Patagonia, AZ 85624. Tel: 520-394-2400.

Southeast of Tucson, this reserve of The Nature Conservancy protects one of the best remaining examples of **riparian wetlands.** A small perennial stream running through the **ciénega** supports a healthy population of an endangered fish. The ciénega is located about 15 mi S of Sonoita on SR-83. LFRW

CANYON DE CHELLY NATIONAL MONUMENT

P.O. Box 588, Chinle, AZ 86503. Tel: 928-674-5500; http://www.nps.gov/cach/

A spectacular canyon incised more than 800 ft into red sandstone of the Colorado Plateau. Navajo farms occupy the floodplain, and many **cliff dwellings** in **alcoves** with numerous **pictographs** and **petroglyphs** are evidence of long human occupation. Canyon walls streaked with **rock varnish** and ancient cliff dwellings can be seen from both the North and South Rim drives. Access to the canyon bottom is by Navajo-guided tours; or from the South Rim, a 2.5 mi round trip hike takes you down to the canyon floor at the foot of White House ruin. LCFRW

CANYONLANDS NATIONAL PARK

2282 S. West Resource Blvd., Moab, UT 84532. Tel: 435-719-2100 (voice), 719-2319 (TTY); http://www.nps.gov/cany

A wilderness of rock at the heart of the Colorado Plateau, in three natural divisions separated by the Green and Colorado River gorges:

1. Maze District. Western sector, one of the most primitive and inaccessible areas of the U.S.A.—a 30-sq-mi sandstone puzzle of **canyons, mesas,** and

buttes, with some notable pictographs. Few visitors. Primarily a 4-wheel drive and hiking experience.

2. Island in the Sky District. NE sector, a broad mesa with rewarding scenic overlooks and a few arches. The most distinctive geological landform is "Upheaval Dome," a jagged-edged crater, possibly created by a meteorite hit or shifting underground salt deposits.

3. Needles District. SE sector, startling landscapes of hoodoos, canyons, arches, joints, grabens (vertical-walled valleys), and potholes. Its "needles" are pinnacles banded in red and white layers. Many unusual arches. Rock art and other traces of aboriginal cultures throughout.

Alert! Fragile, living cryptobiotic soil crust is common in the park—help to protect it by walking only in washes, on rock, and on trails.
CRW(scarce,seasonal)B

CANYONS OF THE ANCIENTS NATIONAL MONUMENT
Established June 2000. BLM Anasazi Heritage Center, 27501 Hwy. 184, Dolores, CO 81328. Tel: 970-882-5600; http://www.co.blm.gov/canm or http://www.co.blm.gov/ahc

The densest concentration of archaeological sites in the nation, with over 6,000 recorded (including dwellings, petroglyphs, hunting camps, and shrines), evidence of cultures and traditions that span thousands of years. The monument is a rugged, natural, backcountry area with no permanent water, few roads, and minimal facilities. Visitors are asked to come to the Anasazi Heritage Center for maps and helpful information (located 3 mi SW of Dolores, CO, on Hwy 184). There are some accessible sites, but visitors need instructions from the Center to navigate unpaved roads that crisscross private property. Follow proper etiquette and Leave No Trace. BP

CAPITOL REEF NATIONAL PARK
HC 70 Box 15, Torrey, UT 84775.
Tel: 435-425-3791;
http://www.nps.gov/care/

Central to this park of colorful cliffs, narrow canyons, ridges and spires is Waterpocket Fold, a sinuous 100-mi-long monocline of tilted and layered rock. Numerous waterpockets (potholes) in the sandstone fill with water during rainstorms. A scenic road (the Burr Trail) crosses over the Fold from Boulder, UT, and then parallels its eastern flank, dipping south to Bullfrog Marina on Lake Powell or north to the park headquarters. Miles of unpaved roads lead into remote areas of natural beauty, including badlands, that offer solitude to park visitors. While there, kindly avoid disturbing areas covered with cryptobiotic soil crust. LCFRWB

CAPULIN VOLCANO NATIONAL MONUMENT
P.O. Box 40, Capulin, NM 88414.
Tel: 505-278-2201;
http://www.nps.gov/cavo/

Located on the western edge of the Great Plains, Capulin Volcano, a nearly perfectly shaped cinder cone, stands more than 1,200 ft above the surrounding plains of northeastern New Mexico. The volcano erupted more than 60,000 years ago. Lava that flowed from the volcano covered almost 16 sq mi. A 2-mi paved road spiraling up to the crater rim makes this one of the most accessible dormant volcanoes in the world. TRW seasonal

Ancient doorways in Pueblo Bonito, Chaco Culture National Historical Park, New Mexico.

CARRIZO PLAIN NATIONAL MONUMENT
Established Jan. 2001. BLM Bakersfield Field Office, 3801 Pegasus Dr., Bakersfield, CA 93308. Tel: 805-475-2131 (Education Center, open Dec. through May); or 661-391-6000 (Field Office); http://www.ca.blm.gov/bakersfield/carrizoplain.html

A place of stark beauty, just 100 mi due W of Los Angeles. Its centerpiece is Soda Lake—a vast winter wetland and a seasonally dry playa of glistening white salts—set in an open grassland rimmed by steep mountains. The San Andreas Fault cuts through the monument, clearly marked by an alignment of ridges, ravines, and pools. The Plain is home to an unusual assemblage of desert plants and animals, with reintroduced Tule elk and pronghorn antelope; the lake attracts thousands of migratory birds. Stop at the Goodwin Education Center for useful information and guided tours—see website for maps and details. LC RBP (very limited lodging available in California Valley)

CATHEDRAL GORGE STATE PARK
P.O. Box 176, Panaca, NV 89042
Tel: 755-728-4460;
www.desertusa.com/nvcat/nvcat.html

In this remote park are amazing examples of erosion—towering, slender, buff-colored spires and columns that reminded early settlers of European cathedrals. Nowhere do the gorge or side ravines exceed depths of 30 ft, but they do resemble slot canyons. Below the escarpment, the soft clay has eroded into a badlands topography. 2 mi N of Panaca on US-93 and 80 mi E of Cedar City, UT. CRW

CEDAR BREAKS NATIONAL MONUMENT
2390 W. Hwy 56, Suite 311, Cedar City, UT 84720. Tel: 435-586-9451;
http://www.go-utah.com/utah/cedar-breaks/information.html

Cedar Breaks, on the west side of the Markagunt Plateau, is a miniature Bryce Canyon—but less crowded. Features fine scenic overlooks, but hiking trails are limited to the rim and upper reaches of the plateau. The single amphitheater, 2,500 ft deep, cuts into colorful siltstone, sandstone, and limestone beds, weathered into

hoodoos. The Visitor Center is located on the rim about 20 mi E of Cedar City and I-15. LFCRW seasonal

CHACO CULTURE NATIONAL HISTORICAL PARK

P. O. Box 220, Nageezi, NM 87037.
Tel: 505-786-7014;
http://www.nps.gov/chcu/

Remote and nestled amongst **mesas** and **buttes** in northeastern New Mexico, Chaco Canyon was a prehistoric urban center of ancestral Pueblo peoples. It's one of America's richest archaeological sites. The park is best known for masterfully engineered architecture on the canyon floor—atop the remains of an ancient sea bed—but there are also small **cliff dwellings** in alcoves near the campground. Dirt access roads from the south are long, rough, and sometimes impassable. It's best to enter the park from the north: turn off US-550 (SR-44) at County Rd. 7900—3 mi SE of Nageezi at Mile Post 112.5. Follow signs to park—5 mi of paved road (CR-7900) and 16 mi of dirt (CR-7950/7985). CRWB

CHIRICAHUA NATIONAL MONUMENT

HC-2, Box 6500, Willcox, AZ 85643.
Tel: 520-824-3560;
http://www.nps.gov/chir/

Explore a fantasy world of towering spires, **hoodoos,** and massive balanced rocks perched delicately on slender pedestals. Called the "Land of the Standing-Up Rocks" by the

Coral Pink Sand Dunes State Park, UT.

Chiricahua Apaches, this small Monument in the southeastern corner of Arizona was formed 27 million years ago by an explosive eruption 1,000 times greater than Mount St. Helens. A winding scenic drive takes you past the Organ Pipe Formation, a sloping cliff face of **volcanic tuff** weathered into rock columns. Several quite strenuous hikes reach the most striking formations. LCRWB

CITY OF ROCKS STATE PARK

P.O. Box 50, Faywood, NM 88034
Tel: 505-536-2800;
http://www.emnrd.state.nm.us/nmparks/
PAGES/PARKS/CITYROCK/
CITYROCK.HTM

Rising from the plains, monoliths eroded from fine **volcanic tuff** suggest mythical monsters, **hoodoos** for sure. Several dozen campsites are scattered among the giant boulders. Walk through the maze of "streets" or clamber over the "houses." Mimbres Indians roamed this area and left arrowheads and potsherds as evidence of their culture. Spanish conquistadors also spent time here, carving **petroglyphs** in the form of crosses into the rocks. CRW

CLAYTON LAKE STATE PARK

Rural Route Box 20, Seneca, NM 88437.
Tel: 505-374-8808;
http://www.emnrd.state.nm.us/nmparks/
PAGES/PARKS/CLAYTON/CLAYTON.htm

Set among rolling grasslands, Clayton Lake State Park features a rocky streambed with more than 500 **fossilized footprints** of plant-eating and carnivorous **dinosaurs** and ancient crocodiles. The best times to view the tracks are in the early morning and late afternoon hours. Located 10-mi NW of Clayton off NM-370. LFCRW

COCHISE STRONGHOLD, AZ *(see Texas Canyon)*

CORAL PINK SAND DUNES STATE PARK

P.O. Box 95, Kanab, UT 84741-0095.
Tel: 435-648-2800;
http://www.stateparks.utah.gov/park_
pages/parkpage.php?id=cpsp

Stunning coral-colored **sand dunes** stretching over 3,730 acres surrounded by sandstone cliffs. In summer, the

Devils Postpile National Monument, CA.

dunes are graced with beautiful displays of long-leaf sunflower and sprawling Welsh's milkweed, a plant found nowhere else. Open year-round, located 12 mi S of US-89 near Kanab. This once-tranquil hideaway now caters to motor homes and dune buggies. CRWB

COYOTE BUTTES *(see Vermilion Cliffs National Monument)*

DEAD HORSE POINT STATE PARK

P.O. Box 609, Moab, UT 84532
Tel: 435-259-2614; http://go-utah.com/
utah/dead-horse-point/state-park.html/

This scenic overlook provides a panoramic view of an enormous bend in the Colorado R. **canyon** 2,000 ft below, the orange-red **cliffs** and **spires** of the canyonlands to the south, and the La Sal Mtns. in the east. Perched on a shelf below the approach road is a **potash mine** with surreal blue evaporation ponds. From Moab take US-191 N to junction with SR-313; head SW on 313 to a signed spur road a few miles before the entrance to Canyonlands National Park. CRW

DEATH VALLEY NATIONAL PARK

P.O. Box 579, Death Valley, CA 92328.
Tel: 760-786-2331;
http://www.nps.gov/deva/

Awe-inspiring scenery, from desolate salt pans to rugged mountains; and plenty of space, 3.3 million acres of it. This showcase of Basin and Range geology offers classic **alluvial fans, bajadas,** colorful **badlands, faults,** ancient **canyons, volcanic features,** and vast **dune fields,** all interwoven with a fascinating human history. A must-see is the maar volcano, **Ubehebe Crater,** not far from historic Scotty's Castle. Badwater, at 282 ft below sea level, is the lowest point in the Western Hemisphere. In the valley, summer daytime highs exceeding 120°F are not unusual; winters are mild and an excellent time to visit. LCFRWB

DEVILS POSTPILE NATIONAL MONUMENT

c/o Sequoia and Kings Canyon National Parks, Three Rivers, CA 93271. Tel: 760-924-5500; http://www.nps.gov/depo/

Stand beside towering **basalt columns** that resemble a stack of giant pencils. Over 900,000 years ago, hot **lava** cooled and cracked to form these slender curved columns, now exposed in a canyon cliff face. Access to the park is by shuttle bus. Nearby are Mammoth Lakes, Hot Creek Gorge Hot Springs, and the heart of the **Long Valley Caldera.** LCFRWB

DINOSAUR NATIONAL MONUMENT

4545 E. Highway 40, Dinosaur, CO 81610-9724. Tel: 970-374-3000; http://www.nps.gov/dino/

Preserved in the sands of an ancient river are **fossils** from the Age of Dinosaurs. At the Visitor Center is an astounding gallery of more than 1,500 bones exposed in a solid rock wall. Outside, the landscape is no less interesting—200,000 acres of colorful **hogback ridges, plateaus,** and **canyons** surround the confluence of the Green and Yampa Rivers. The canyons differ in character from those at Canyonlands and the Grand Canyon—many rocky layers have been squeezed, twisted, and faulted. Throughout the park is elaborate **rock art** created by the prehistoric Fremont people. CFRWB

EL MALPAIS NATIONAL MONUMENT

123 E. Roosevelt, Grants, NM 87020.
Tel: El Malpais Information Ctr. 505-783-4774; **Monument Headquarters** 505-285-4641; http://www.nps.gov/elma/

El Malpais (the bad country) is a broad and windswept land of ancient **lava flows** and sprawling forests of pine and aspen. I-40 crosses the northern margin, but the landscape is best viewed along SR-117, which runs south along the edge of the Monument. This park contains one of the longest **lava tube** systems in North America. Stop at the Northwest New Mexico Visitor Center (tel: 505-876-2783) at I-40 Exit 85 for information; the park's smaller Information Center is located on SR-53. Nearby is the Candelaria **Ice Cave** (on private land), a lava tube which contains permanent ice all year. For a small fee, you can walk into the cave (no flashlight needed) and skirt the edge of **Bandera Crater,** an impressive cinder cone. RB

EL MORRO NATIONAL MONUMENT

Route 2, Box 43, Ramah, NM 87321.
Tel: 505-783-4226;
http://www.nps.gov/elmo/

For centuries, beginning long before Columbus stepped ashore, travelers have carved **petroglyphs** and inscriptions into this 200-ft-high sandstone **mesa.** Atop the monolith—a 2-mi round-trip hike up a paved trail— Pueblo Indian ruins provide another glimpse into the past. Located 56 mi SE of Gallup, NM, via SR-602 to SR-53; or 42 mi SW of Grants, NM, via SR-53. LCFRW

FLORISSANT FOSSIL BEDS NATIONAL MONUMENT

P. O. Box 185, Florissant, CO 80816-0185. Tel: 719-748-3253;
http://www.nps.gov/flfo/index.htm

This park offers a glimpse of life in central Colorado 34-35 million years ago. A rain of fine volcanic ash preserved hundreds of species of delicate insects—a rarity—and more than 140 kinds of plants, along with a few birds and mammals such as mesohippus (an ancestor to the modern horse). While most of the fossils are now housed in museums worldwide, some are on display in the Visitor Center. Winding through ponderosa pine forest and mountain meadows are 14 mi of scenic trails; short ones lead to petrified redwood stumps and an 1878 homestead. LFRW

GILA CLIFF DWELLINGS NATIONAL MONUMENT

HC-68, Box 100, Silver City NM 88061.
Tel: 505-536-9461;
http://www.nps.gov/gicl/

Five natural **alcoves** weathered from an overhanging cliff face of coarse conglomerate high above the canyon floor provide the setting for these ruins. Late in the 13th century, people of the **Mogollon culture** built this complex of about 40 rooms. Most of these cliff dwellings are accessible through a self-guided 1-mi loop trail that leads from the parking lot to the ruins. The trail is unpaved and a steep 180-foot climb without handrails. Ranger-guided tours are also available. The ruins lie 45 mi N of Silver City via SR-15, a 2-hour drive. LCFRWB

GLEN CANYON NATIONAL RECREATION AREA

P.O. Box 1507, Page AZ 86040.
Tel: 928-608-6404;
http://www.nps.gov/glca/

Mostly in Utah, this wonderland of red and orange sandstone cradles **Lake Powell,** the second largest man-made lake in the USA, formed in 1963 by Glen Canyon Dam on the Colorado R. Its sparkling blue water attracts people from afar for fishing, water sports, and houseboating in the desert. Cliffs boldly streaked with **rock varnish** and numerous **prehistoric ruins** and **rock art** can be seen along the lakeshore. Several **slot canyons,** natural **arches,** and **Rainbow Bridge Nat'l Monument** (see Rainbow Bridge listing) are also accessible by boat. LCFRWB

Remnant of an ancient fossil reef in Guadalupe Mountains National Park, TX. Photo by William Dupré.

GOBLIN VALLEY STATE PARK

P.O. Box 637, Green River, UT 84525.
Tel: 435-564-3633

Water and wind have sculpted thousands of chocolate-colored sandstone monoliths into fantastical **hoodoos**, resembling mushrooms, cartoon characters, and other fanciful creatures—a delightful excursion for photographers, and children of all ages. This remote park has been recently enlarged and features hundreds of dirt roads to explore in 4WD vehicles. CRWB

GOOSENECKS STATE PARK

660 W. 400 N., Blanding, UT 84511.
Tel: 435-678-2238;
http://www.stateparks.utah.gov/park_pages/scenicparkpage.php?id=gnsp

Look down into a 1,000-foot **canyon** carved by the San Juan R. as it **meanders** sluggishly towards the Colorado R. and Lake Powell. Its path obstructed by a maze of narrow gooseneck-like panels of rock (as seen from above), the river flows for nearly 6 mi to cover just one straight mile as the crow flies. Located 4 mi off SR-261, near Mexican Hat. CRB

GRAND CANYON NATIONAL PARK

P.O. Box 129, Grand Canyon, AZ 86023.
Tel: 928-638-7888;
http://www.nps.gov/grca/

Truly one of the great wonders of the world. Here, on the **Colorado Plateau**, over 2 billion years of Earth's history are exposed in the **canyon** walls—the clearest profile of geo-time to be seen anywhere. Explore this scenic chasm by car, by boat, by plane, by mule, or by foot. Most visitors are content to follow the scenic rim drives—the South Rim is open all year, the North Rim, which is higher, cooler and less visited, is closed during the winter months. For current information on accommodations, recreational options, and fees, call ahead or visit the park's comprehensive website. LCFRWB

GRAND CANYON–PARASHANT NATIONAL MONUMENT

Established Jan. 2000. BLM Arizona Strip Field Office, 345 E. Riverside Dr., St. George, UT 84790. Tel: 435-688-3246;
http://www.az.blm.gov/parashant.htm or
http://www.nps.gov/para

Jointly administered by the BLM and the NPS, this remote geological treasure in NW Arizona borders Grand Canyon National Park to the south and the state of Nevada to the west, encompassing a bit of Lake Mead National Recreation Area. Canyon walls expose ancient beds of **sedimentary rock** along the edge of the **Colorado Plateau**. And **volcanic features**—some only 1,000 years old—populate the area (see p. 123). The monument also protects archaeological sites and a diverse flora and fauna, ranging from Joshua trees and desert tortoises in lowlands to ponderosa pines and Kaibab squirrels upon the plateau. No visitor facilities, and cell phones won't work here. Primitive roads; two spare tires recommended. Get a map from the BLM website or office in St. George. BP

GRAND FALLS

Little Colorado River; Cameron Visitor Center (at Jct. US-64 & US-89), P. O. Box 459, Cameron, AZ 86020.
Tel: 928-679-2303.

During spring snowmelt or after a summer storm, see a **waterfall** higher than Niagara. **Lava** from a volcanic eruption about 100,000 years ago dammed the Little Colorado R. channel, forcing the river to take a detour over the **plateau** before dropping back into the gorge. Eight miles E of Flagstaff, take the Camp Townsend-Winona Rd. to Leupp Rd., turn left. Proceed for 15 mi just past a cinder mine to a sign that says Grand Falls Bible Church, 1 mi. To reach the overlook, turn left on Indian Route 70, a 9-mi. dirt road—very muddy when wet. Drive and hike with caution! The Navajo welcome visitors to Grand Falls, but a back-country permit (available at Cameron Visitor Center) is required for travel off the main route. PicnicArea+RB

GRAND STAIRCASE-ESCALANTE NATIONAL MONUMENT

Kanab Visitor Center: 745 E. Hwy 89, Kanab, UT 84741. Tel: 435-644-4680. Escalante Visitor Center: 755 W. Main, Escalante, UT 84726. Tel: 435-826-5499;
http://www.ut.blm.gov/monument/

If you are looking for solitude, explore this newly created park: 1.9 million acres of rugged **canyons**, multi-hued **cliffs, plateaus, mesas,** and **badlands** bordered by Capitol Reef and Bryce Canyon National Parks and Glen Canyon National Recreation Area. Divided into three distinct regions:

1. Grand Staircase. A series of great scenic steps that ascend northward across the southwest corner of the Monument, defined by the Chocolate, Vermilion, White, Gray, and Pink Cliffs;

2. Kaiparowits Plateau. A vast wedge-shaped block of mesas and deeply incised canyons, much of it forested. Flanking the SW edge of the Plateau is the Cockscomb, a spectacular **monocline** reached via the Cottonwood Canyon Rd. just N of US-89.

3. Canyons of the Escalante. A magical labyrinth of interconnected canyons—including many **slot canyons**—that drain the southern flank of the Aquarius Plateau into the Escalante R.

Nearly all roads are unpaved and primitive, and don't count on finding any water or services in this vast Monument. Plan carefully. Hike with care too—there's much fragile

cryptobiotic soil crust in the park. P +2 small campgrounds - LFRW (in surrounding communities)

GRAPEVINE CANYON

about 8 mi from Laughlin, NV
http://www.desertusa.com/spirit/du_spritmt.html

Features one of the largest collections of rock art in Nevada. Boulders near the mouth of the canyon are covered with Native American **petroglyphs** believed to be about 800 years old. A small desert spring flows here year-round, an oasis for wildlife. To get there, take SR-163 W from Laughlin for about 6 mi to the Christmas Tree Pass turnoff. Follow this dirt road N for 2-3 mi—look for a short side road on your left that ends in a large parking area. A trail leads up a wash to the site, a 5-min walk. Photograph the petroglyphs, but please don't touch. P

GREAT SALT LAKE: ANTELOPE ISLAND STATE PARK

4528 West 1700 South, Syracuse, UT 84075. Tel: 801-725-9263 or 773-2941; http://www.utah.com/places/state_parks/antelope_island.htm

This small remnant of prehistoric Lake Bonneville (see Bonneville Salt Flats) is the largest natural lake west of the Mississippi R. and the world's fourth largest lake with no outlet. It averages 1,700 sq mi in area and 20 ft in depth, is usually 3-5 times saltier than the ocean, and contains no fish. The lake serves as a fueling station for hundreds of thousands of migrating birds that feed on its bounty of brine shrimp and brine flies. Its beach sand is unique: tiny, brown-to-white, egg-like grains, called **oolites**, layers of calcium built around a central core (a mineral fragment or brine shrimp fecal pellet). Salt, magnesium, and potash are mined here; and a 1,200-ft smoke stack sits on the south shore, part of an enormous copper smelting operation. To bask in the sun or explore by foot, bicycle, car, or sailboat, take the causeway (from I-15 use Exit #335 near Layton) to **Antelope Island State Park.** Introduced herds of bison, elk, and pronghorn antelope populate this unusual island. LFCRW

GREAT SAND DUNES NATIONAL MONUMENT

11500 Highway 150, Mosca, CO 81146.
Tel: 719-378-2312;
http://www.nps.gov/grsa/

Hugging the western slope of the Sangre de Cristo Mountains are golden sand dunes over 750 ft tall, the tallest in the USA. There are two approach roads: E from Mosca or from the S along SR-150. Because sand temperature can quickly reach 140° F in summer, when hiking, don't forget your shoes! LFCRW

GUADALUPE MOUNTAINS NATIONAL PARK

HC 60 Box 400, Salt Flat, TX 79847.
Tel: 915-828-3251; http://nps.gov/gumo/

Rising from the desert floor, 110 mi E of El Paso, the Guadalupe Mtns. contain remnants of an ancient **fossil reef**, among the best examples on Earth. This reef formed from limy accumulations of plant and animal skeletons in a Permian sea; to see it up-close, take the Permian Reef Geology Trail. Hiking is the best way to explore this vast wilderness, and here you can hike to the highest point in Texas, Guadalupe Peak, at 8,749 ft. In McKittrick Canyon, you'll find a spring-fed stream, **travertine flows,** and luxuriant plant life that's especially colorful in autumn. And **gypsum dunes** flank the Western Escarpment. The park is open year-round—with hot summers and mild winters. Sudden and extreme weather changes are common, so when hiking prepare for the unexpected. CRWB

HAVASU CANYON

c/o Havasupai Tourist Enterprise, P. O. Box 160, Supai, AZ 86435.
Tel: 928-448-2121 or 448-2731;
http://www.great-adventures.com/destinations/usa/arizona/havasu.html

A remote and scenic branch of the Grand Canyon—home of the Havasupai, "people of the blue-green waters." Along its 10-mi course to the Colorado R., Havasu Creek plunges over four stunning **waterfalls** flanked by **travertine** mineral deposits (see text). The hot and rigorous 8-mi hike from the south rim of the Grand Canyon to the village of Supai on the canyon floor is worth the effort; more expensive alternatives are renting horses or traveling there by helicopter. The trail begins at Hualapai Hilltop, a parking area with no facilities; the nearest town is Peach Springs, 68 mi away on SR-66. Facilities in the canyon are few, and hiking permits are required in advance. Havasu Falls is 2 mi down-canyon from Supai. Be courteous and sensitive to the ways of the Havasupai. LCFRW

HOOVER DAM (see Lake Mead National Recreation Area)

HOPI MESAS

c/o Hopi Tribal Headquarters, P. 0. Box 123, Kykotsmovi, AZ 86039.
Tel: 928-734-2445

The traditional villages of the Hopi are perched on three **mesas** in northern Arizona—First, Second, and Third Mesa, from east to west respectively. They lie just off SR-264 between Tuba City and Window Rock. Plan to visit the Hopi Cultural Center on Second Mesa. To visit other villages, stop at the town hall, register, and a native guide will show you around. No photography is permitted. LFRW

HORSESHOE BEND SCENIC OVERLOOK

For information, contact the John Wesley Powell Memorial Museum & Visitor Center, P.O. Box 547, Page, AZ 86040.
Tel: 928-645-9496 or 888-597-6873;
http://powellmuseum.org/index.html

One of the most breath-taking overlooks above the Colorado R., a tight bend in the **Glen Canyon gorge** not far below the dam. The trailhead is poorly marked but easy to find: about 3 mi S of Page along US-89, look for

a turnoff to a dirt parking area below a low sandy bluff just west of the highway between Mileposts 544 & 545. The walk to the cliff edge is 1.5 mi round-trip in loose sand and rock. There are no guard rails along the sheer dropoff—not for the faint-of-heart. Tour guides are available in Page. LCF

HUECO TANKS
STATE HISTORICAL PARK

6900 Hueco Tanks Road No. 1, El Paso, TX 79938. Tel: 915-857-1135; http://www.tpwd.state.tx.us/park/hueco/hueco.htm

Named for the area's natural rock basins (**huecos** in Spanish) that trap rainwater. Early Americans, as well as later tribes, camped by the waterholes and painted numerous **pictographs** on nearby rocks. Later, the site was a stop on the Butterfield Overland Mail Route, and the park contains the ruins of the stagecoach station. To reach the park, take US-62/180, 32 mi E of El Paso, then turn N on Ranch Rd 2775. Restricted access—to see the best pictographs, you must sign up for a ranger-guided tour; call ahead. CRW

IRONWOOD FOREST
NATIONAL MONUMENT

Established June 2000. BLM Tucson Field Office, 12661 E. Broadway, Tucson, AZ 85748. Tel: 520-258-7200; http://www.az.blm.gov/ironwood/ironwood.htm or http://arizona.sierraclub.org/monuments

A **Basin and Range** geo-region that sustains an extraordinary diversity of Sonoran Desert plant and animal life, including impressive forests of saguaro cacti and ironwood trees. The ironwood is forage and cover for nearly 150 species of birds, 62 species of reptiles and amphibians, and 64 kinds of mammals; and more than 230 plant species are known to start their growth under ironwood "nurse plants." Three of the monument's four mountain ranges are **volcanic** in origin; the fourth, the Waterman range, is sedimentary, much of it **limestone**. The Silverbell Mountains are mined for **copper**. The area also contains significant cultural and historical sites, some dating back 5,000 years. Located 25 mi NW of Tucson and an hour's drive S of Phoenix. Access from I-10; best to download a map from website. No facilities. Day use and 4-wheel drive recommended—no off-roading. FBP

JOSHUA TREE NATIONAL PARK

74485 National Park Drive, 29 Palms, CA 92277. Tel: 760-367-5500; http://www.nps.gov/jotr/

This park's diverse topography offers desert life in a spectacular geological setting, a rugged **Basin & Range** environment with **canyons, alluvial fans, bajadas,** and **playas.** In the high country are strange, spiky Joshua trees—a type of yucca—and odd piles of huge monzogranite boulders; in wandering amongst them, look for **hoodoos, arches,** and **tinajas.** The park's five fan-palm **oases** are meccas for wildlife. And from Keys View, one of the highest peaks in the park, the line of the **San Andreas Fault** is detectable. LCFRWB

KASHA–KATUWE TENT ROCKS
NATIONAL MONUMENT

Established Jan. 2001. BLM Albuquerque Field Office, 435 Montaño Rd. NE, Albuquerque, NM 87107. Tel: 505-761-8700; http://www.nm.blm.gov/aufo/tent_rocks/tent_rocks.html

A unique geological area between Albuquerque and Santa Fe. Kasha–Katuwe means *white cliffs* in Keresan, the traditional language for the Pueblo de Cochiti. The area

Organ Pipe Cactus National Monument, AZ.

features large, ten-shaped rocks/ **hoodoos** and canyons, erosional features that emerged from a 400-ft-thick bed of **volcanic** debris (mostly ash/**tuff** and pumice) deposited during the last million years. The rock is soft and fragile—no climbing, please! To get there, take I-25 to Cochiti Reservoir Exit to SR-22 (or SR-16 to SR-22); follow signs to Cochiti Pueblo. Turn right onto Tribal Route 92 at the pueblo water tower (painted like a drum) and Forest Service Rd 266, an improved road; parking is 5 mi ahead. Day use only for picnicking and hiking; take your trash with you. Dogs must be kept on leash. No collecting of any kind. FRP

KELSO DUNES

Mojave National Preserve Desert Information Center, 72157 Baker Blvd./ PO Box 241, Baker, CA 92309. Tel: 760-733-4040; http://wrgis.wr.usgs.gov/docs/parks/ mojave/kelso1.html

The quartz sand of this 25,000 year-old **dune field** arrived on winds from the Mojave R. Sink near Afton Canyon. Under the right conditions, you can hear a distinctive booming when sand slides down the dune faces. Plants have stabilized some dunes. The field lies W of Kelbaker Rd., which connects I-15 and I-40. Open to hikers, but closed to vehicles. RP

KODACHROME BASIN STATE PARK

P. O. Box 238, Cannonville, UT 84718. Tel: 435-679-8562; http://www.go-utah.com/utah/ kodachrome-state-park/Kodachrome.html

Named in 1948 by the leaders of a National Geographic expedition— after Kodachrome film, which excelled in capturing the brilliant red hues of the park's cliffs and **hoodoos.** Unique to this park is a collection of 67 **sand pipes** ("chimney rocks"), oddly shaped rock pillars that rise 6-170 ft. Their origin remains a mystery, though they seem to be the hardened remains of ancient springs and geysers that filled with sediment. LCFRW

LAKE MEAD NATIONAL RECREATION AREA

601 Nevada Hwy., Boulder City, NV 89005. Tel: 702-293-8990; http://www.nps.gov/lame/

The first major dam on the Colorado R., named Boulder Dam and later renamed Hoover Dam. The huge reservoir behind the dam, Lake Mead, is 110 mi long and has 550 mi of shoreline, an enormously popular recreation area which attracts visitors mainly interested in water sports and fishing. Most of the park is rugged desert—the meeting ground of the Sonoran, Mojave, and Great Basin desert regions—and offers a rich variety of plant and animal life. LFCRW

LAVA RIVER CAVE

Peaks Ranger District, Coconino National Forest, 5075 N. Hwy 89, Flagstaff, AZ 86004. Tel: 928-526-0866.

For the intrepid explorer, hike into the guts of a **lava tube.** Lava River Cave lies in the San Francisco Volcanic Field. To reach the cave take US-180 N to Milepost 230; turn left onto Forest Service Road 245 and travel W for 3 mi to FS Rd 171. Continue S on 171 and then left on 171B for 1 mi to the cave. Extra flashlights, sturdy shoes, warm clothes and a hard hat are highly recommended. LFCRW

LITTLE PAINTED DESERT NAVAJO COUNTY PARK

P. O. Box 668, Holbrook, AZ 86025. Tel. 928-524-4251.

A quiet alternative to—and about 54 mi W of—the Painted Desert at Petrified Forest Nat'l Park. About 660 acres of colorful **badlands** with no marked trails and plenty of hiking opportunities. Exit I-40 at Exit 257 & take SR-87 N for 15 mi to sign. Free admission. PicnicArea+R

MAMMOTH LAKES AND LONG VALLEY

Mammoth Lakes Visitors Bureau, P.O. Box 48, Mammoth Lakes, CA 93546. Tel: 1-800-367-6572; http://visitmammoth.com

The area's breathtaking scenery tells a story of tremendous earthquakes and explosive volcanoes, shaping and reshaping the face of the Earth. An ominous bulge in the center of Long Valley Caldera continues to grow,

pumped up by fresh injections of magma. Since 1994, large stands of 300-year-old trees on the edge of the caldera have been dying, killed by carbon dioxide upwelling in the soil. Take the self-guided Volcanic Auto Tour, and in just a few miles see **craters, cones,** and steaming **hot springs;** start from Lee Vining or Mammoth Lakes. LFCW

MESA VERDE NATIONAL PARK

P.O. Box 8, Mesa Verde National Park, CO 81330. Tel: 970-529-4465; http://www.nps.gov/meve

Mesa Verde's **canyons, cliffs,** and **mesas** hold evidence of more than 700 years of human occupation, including ancestral homes of Pueblo Indians. Cliff Palace contains more than 150 rooms in a single enormous **alcove.** Many enlightening scenic overlooks are accessible by car. The agile and adventurous should try self-guided tours—some require climbing. For a close look at other sites, ranger-guided tours are available; but much of the mesa is closed to the public for conservation reasons. LCFRW

"METEOR" CRATER

Meteor Crater Enterprises, P.O. Box 70, Flagstaff, AZ 86002-0070. Tel: 928-289-2362; Headquarters 800-289-5898; http://barringercrater.com/

For those fascinated by falling objects from outer space, this is a must-see attraction. It's a hole large enough for 20 football fields. The Barringer family owns the site, on lease to Meteor Crater Enterprises. One can view this 570-ft-deep meteorite crater from three different lookout posts or take a guided hike along the rim. The crater can be reached by taking Exit 233 on I-40, 40 mi E of Flagstaff. FRW

MOJAVE NATIONAL PRESERVE

222 E. Main St., Suite 202, Barstow, CA 92311. Baker Information Center Tel: 760-733-4040; http://www.nps.gov/moja/

An expanse of rugged mountains, volcanic **cinder cones, lava flows, ghost towns** and colorful **sand dunes,** on 1.6 million acres of Mojave desert, extremely hot in summer and surprisingly cold in winter. On a dry day, stop by the **Kelso Dunes** and listen for **booming sands.** P(mostly)

MONAHANS SANDHILLS STATE PARK

Box 1738, Monahans, TX 79756.
Tel: 915-943-2092;
http://www.tpwd.state.tx.us/park/
monahans/monahans.htm

Once covered by a Permian sea, this 3,840-acre expanse of silica sand dunes (some up to 70-ft high) is about a 30-minute drive west of Odessa. The park includes a blend of active and stabilized dunes, part of a dune system that reaches into eastern New Mexico. Shifting sand has uncovered bones of extinct camels and mastodons here. Windows at the Visitors Center offer opportunities to view birds and other wildlife attracted by offerings of food and water. LFCRW

MONO LAKE TUFA STATE RECREATION AREA

P.O. Box 99, Lee Vining, CA 93541.
http://cal-parks.ca.gov/
default.asp?page_id=514

Strange, yet exquisite **tufa towers** protrude from the salty water of Mono Lake, one of the oldest lakes in North America and perhaps the busiest international airport for water birds in California. The water feels slippery—it's 80 times more alkaline than seawater. Since 1941, lake levels have been dropping due to water diversions from tributary streams to supply cities in southern California. A Tufa Reserve was created in 1981 to preserve this geological treasure—located 10 mi SE of Lee Vining via US-395. Also, the two prominent islands in Mono Lake and the nearby Mono Craters are **volcanoes** that erupted within the last 1,000 years. LCFRWB

MONTEZUMA CASTLE NATIONAL MONUMENT

Box 219, Camp Verde, AZ 86322.
Tel: 928-567-3322;
http://www.nps.gov/moca/

Visit one of the best-preserved **cliff dwellings** in North America. This 5-story, 20-room cliff house built by the Sinagua Indians about 900 years ago is nestled in a limestone **alcove** high above the flood plain of Beaver Creek in the Verde Valley. A level, self-guided trail passes beneath the ruins, but due to its fragility, entry is prohibited.

An excellent trailside diorama brings this Sinagua dwelling to life. Located 5 mi NE of Camp Verde; take Exit 289 from I-17. And just to the north is Montezuma Well, a small **spring**-fed lake in an ancient limestone sink-hole, once used for irrigation by Sinagua and Hohokam farmers. LCFRW

MONUMENT VALLEY

Superintendent, Box 360289, Monument Valley, UT 84536. Tel: 435-727-3287;
http://www.americansouthwest.net/utah/
monument_valley/

No other landscape of the American West is as indelibly etched in the public mind as this desolate yet breathtakingly beautiful valley. Isolated mesas, buttes, and spires surrounded by open sandy desert have been the setting for countless western movies and advertisements. The area is entirely within the Navajo Indian Reservation on the UT/AZ border. Views from the Visitor Center are spectacular but to really get a feel for the park take the 17-mi, 4WD loop drive. Or take a guided tour through Mystery Valley to see several **arches, cliff dwellings** and **rock art.** On the drive south to Kayenta, Agathla Peak, a jagged volcanic neck, rises sharply above the plains And about 6 mi E of Kayenta by US-160 is Church Rock, another impressive **volcanic neck.** LCFRW+B(with Navajo guides)

MULESHOE NATIONAL WILDLIFE REFUGE

P.O. Box 549, Muleshoe, TX 79347.
Tel: 806-946-3341;
http://southwest.fws.gov/refuges/texas/
muleshoe/index.html

Situated on short-grass prairies of west Texas, Muleshoe was the first national wildlife refuge in the state. Look for wintering sandhill cranes on these **playa lakes**—one of the largest populations in North America—and other migratory waterfowl that frequent this stop on the central flyway. From the town of Muleshoe, take SR-214 S 20 mi, then go W on Caliche Road for 2.25 mi. CRW

MYSTERY VALLEY, AZ (see Monument Valley)

NATURAL BRIDGES NATIONAL MONUMENT

HC 60, Box 1, Lake Powell, UT 84533.
Tel: 435-692-1234;
http//www.nps.gov/nabr/

Meandering intermittent streams have cut through sandstone walls and created three large **natural bridges** in a high desert setting. Bridge Drive is a 9-mi one-way loop road that will take you to overlooks of all three bridges and a small ancestral Pueblo (Anasazi) ruin. For a closer look, hike to them; some of the trails are easy; others are more challenging but are aided by short ladders. Climbing on the bridges is prohibited. Along the way, you'll see **hanging gardens** on the canyon walls and prehistoric rock art. Cliffs are sheer and most drop-offs are unfenced. A more modern attraction is the Photovoltaic Array, one of the largest solar power generators in the world, reached by a short trail starting near the Visitor Center. CRB

NAVAJO NATIONAL MONUMENT

HC-71, Box 3, Tonalea, AZ 86044-9704.
Tel: 928-672-2366;
http://www.nps.gov/nava/

This Monument features two elaborate **cliff dwellings**—Betatakin and Keet Seel—in a magnificent canyon setting. Abandoned by ancient Pueblo people (the Anasazi) more than six centuries ago, both ruins are nestled in sandstone **alcoves.** An easy trail leads to an overlook of Betatakin—but for a closer look, you'll need a park ranger escort; tours depart daily at 8:00 AM, limited to 25, first come, first serve. A visit to Keet Seel requires a backcountry permit; daily visits are limited to 20 persons, so plan ahead. Open from Memorial Day through Labor Day weekend. This Monument is on private Navajo land, and visitors are not free to wander on their own. FCRW seasonal

NEWSPAPER ROCK

BLM Field Office, 435 N. Main St.,
Monticello, UT 84535.
Tel: 435-587-1500;
http://www.blm.gov/utah/monticello/
camping.htm

On the drive into the Needles District of Canyonlands National Park, on

SR-211, stop at this rock art panel—among the best in the Southwest. Navajos call it Tse Hane, rock that tells a story. In fact, about 2,000 years of graphic story-telling are recorded here as **petroglyphs,** starting with prehistoric peoples—probably from the Archaic, Basketmaker, Fremont, and Pueblo cultures—and continued into historic times, with contributions from Navajo tribesmen and Anglos. CR

ORGAN PIPE CACTUS NATIONAL MONUMENT

Route 1, Box 100, Ajo, AZ 85321.
Tel: 520-387-6849;
http://www.nps.gov/orpi/

Sitting right on the Arizona-Mexico border in the **Basin and Range** is a ruggedly beautiful volcanic landscape of mountains, canyons, and **bajadas** studded with columnar cacti. Saguaro cacti abound and it's the northernmost limit for the less cold-tolerant organ pipe cactus. To explore this heartland of the Sonoran Desert, take the 53-mi Puerto Blanco Drive to the west or the 21-mi Ajo Mountain Drive to the east. These one-way loop roads are unpaved and not recommended for RV's or caravans. Another attraction within the park is Quitobaquito Spring, a site of great historical interest and an oasis for wildlife. LFCRWB

PALATKI CLIFF DWELLINGS *(see Sedona, AZ)*

PALO DURO CANYON STATE PARK

RR 2 - Box 285, Canyon, TX 79015.
Tel: 806-488-2227;
http://www.tpwd.state.tx.us/park/
paloduro/paloduro.htm

During the past one million years, a fork of the Red River carved this colorful, rugged 110-mi-long, 800-ft-deep chasm in the high plains of western Texas. Geologically, this is a relatively young canyon—its oldest layers at the bottom are about the same age as the youngest layers at the top of the Grand Canyon, a mere 250 million years old! Towering cliffs are banded in red, yellow, purple, and white; red clay and veins of white gypsum blanket the ground. The park's trails serve hikers, runners, mountain bikers, and

Sagging sediments in Red Rock Canyon State Park, CA.

equestrians. A 5-mi roundtrip leads to the Lighthouse, a 75-ft high shale and sandstone **pinnacle.**
L (very limited) FCRWB

PARIA CANYON-VERMILION CLIFFS WILDERNESS *(see Vermilion Cliffs National Monument)*

PETROGLYPH NATIONAL MONUMENT

6001 Unser Boulevard, NW,
Albuquerque, NM 87120.
Tel: 505-899-0205;
http://desertusa.com/pnm/pnm.html

More than 20,000 prehistoric and historic Native American and Hispanic **petroglyphs** stretch 17 mi along Albuquerque's West Mesa escarpment. You can visit three areas within the 11-sq-mi park: Boca Negra, Rinconada Canyon, and Piedras Marcadas. Rock art is concentrated in the first two sites; and Piedras Marcadas, formerly known as Volcano Park, features **lava flows** and five **cinder cones.** If traveling on I-40, take the Unser Blvd. Exit N 3 mi to Visitor Center; it's 5 mi N to Boca Negra. LFRW

PETRIFIED FOREST NATIONAL PARK

P.O. Box 2217, Petrified Forest Nat'l Park, AZ 86028. Tel: 928-524-6228;
http://www.nps.gov/pefo/

Though petrified wood is widespread in the West, this park protects and showcases one of the world's richest and most colorful deposits. But that's not all. Here paleontologists have discovered a remarkable assemblage of

other **fossils** that have aided our understanding of life on Earth late in the Triassic period. Exciting reconstructions of giant amphibians and reptiles of the times are on display at the Rainbow Forest Museum. Outside, see for yourself how these agatized logs emerge from the **Painted Desert badlands** terrain. Archaeological sites and **petroglyphs** are scattered throughout the park. LFRWB

PICACHO PEAK STATE PARK

P. O. Box 275, Picacho, AZ 85241.
Tel: 520-466-3183;
http://www.desertusa.com/azpicacho/
azpicacho.html

A small desert park with a prominent landmark, Picacho Peak, a 1,500-ft tilted remnant of ancient lava flows capped by a large block of Precambrian **granite.** Enthusiastic hikers enjoy the climb to its top. After wet, mild winters, slopes at the base of the peak are carpeted with wildflowers, enough to stop traffic. The showy Mexican gold poppy prefers copper-rich soils, often common in volcanic areas. Between Tucson and Phoenix, just off I-10, with 95 campsites. FCRW

PINACATE BIOSPHERE RESERVE

Sonora, Mexico: Reserva de La Biosfera El Pinacate y El Gran Desierto de Altar. Access from Mexico's Route 2 at KM Post 51, 32 mi W of Sonoyta; or from Route 8, 32 mi SW of Sonoyta at KM Post 52.

Only hardy souls seeking adventure, beauty, and discovery should consider an expedition to this desolate land of **cinder cones, lava flows,** and giant

maar craters. Over 400 cinder cones that erupted 2,000 to 1 million years ago are scattered across a 600-sq-mi expanse of Sonoran Desert. West and south of the volcanic area lie golden sands of the Gran Desierto de Altar, the largest **sea of sand** in North America. Ideal times to visit are between November and March. The Pinacate area is dangerously remote and undeveloped, and it's unwise to travel there alone. If you go, take plenty of drinking water, spare car parts, and common sense. Before entering the reserve, register with the Reserve Office at KM Post 52 on Route 8. P

PIPE SPRING
NATIONAL MONUMENT

HC 65 Box 5, Fredonia, AZ 86022. Tel: 928-643-7105; http://www.nps.gov/pisp/

An oasis in the desert with four springs in the area that rise from the Sevier Fault on Hurricane Ridge.

Ancestral Pueblo and Paiute Indians were the first people drawn here. Later, Mormon settlers attracted by the water and grasslands established ranches. This historical site is located 14 mi W of Fredonia on the Arizona strip, a 12,000-sq-mi region in northern Arizona, N of the Grand Canyon and S of the Utah border. FRW

PYRAMID LAKE

P.O. Box 256, Nixon, NV 89424; Ranger Station Tel: 775-476-1155; or BLM, Carson City Field Office, 5665 Morgan Mill Road, Carson City, NV 89701; Tel: 775-476-1156; http://www.nevadaweb. com/cnt/r-t/pyramid/main.html

Explorer John C. Frémont, named this lake for a huge tufa tower that resembles an Egyptian pyramid, and many odd **tufa needles and domes** line the shore. This is the largest natural lake in Nevada, a remnant of Lake Lahontan, which covered parts of NV and CA during the Pleistocene. It attracts flocks of migrating birds, along with nesting white pelicans. A

Paiute Indian reservation encloses the lake. To explore the many unmarked access roads, inquire at the Ranger Station in the Paiute community of Sutcliffe on the lake's west shore. Located 33 mi NE of Reno on Pyramid Lake Hwy (SR-445); 14 mi N of I-80. LCFR

RAINBOW BASIN
NATURAL AREA

Barstow BLM Field Office, 2601 Barstow Rd., CA 92311. Tel: 760-252-6000; http://www.ca.blm.gov/barstow/ basin.html

A diverse landscape of scenic canyons and multicolored rock formations—a great display of layered, folded, and tilted rocks; the basin is a classic example of a **syncline.** The area is rich in fossils, but a permit is required to collect them. To get there from Barstow, go N on First Ave., turn left on Irwin Rd., then left on Fossil Bed Rd. and follow signs. LCFRW

Chapel of the Holy Cross, Sedona, AZ.

RAINBOW BRIDGE
NATIONAL MONUMENT

P.O. Box 1507, Page, AZ 86040.
Tel: 520-608-6404; http://nps.gov/rabr/

Home to the world's largest **natural bridge,** a 275 ft (84 m) span that's 290 ft (88 m) high. Public access is by boat across Lake Powell—tours depart from Wahweap Marina near Page year-round, and during the summer, tours are also available from Bullfrog and Halls Crossing marinas. Back-packers need permits from the Navajo Nation; write to Navajo Nation, Parks & Recreation Dept., Box 9000, Window Rock, AZ 86515. LFRWB

RED CANYON

Powell Ranger District, P. O. Box 80, Panguitch, UT 84759.
Tel: 435-676-8815;
http://www.fs.fed.us/dxnf/campground/indexpo.html

Situated near the gateway to Bryce Canyon along Scenic Byway 12, with similar rock formations and plenty of **hoodoos.** The Pink Ledges Trail is an easy, photogenic 20-minute loop that starts at the Visitor Center (tel: 435-676-2676, seasonal). The Red Canyon area is home to almost a dozen plants known only in this vicinity, including ten dwarf wildflowers. LCFRWB seasonal

RED ROCK CANYON
STATE PARK

Angeles District, Mojave Desert Sector, 43779 15th St. West, Lancaster, CA 93534. Tel: 661-942-0662;
http://cal-parks.ca.gov/default.asp?page_id=631

A series of multi-hued desert **canyons** and **buttes** with scenic cliff faces of exposed lake sediments and volcanic deposits eroded into **badlands.** Fossil mammal bones have been found here. Located along SR-14, 25 mi N of Mojave. CRWB

RIO GRANDE
WILD AND SCENIC RIVER

BLM, Taos Field Office, 226 Cruz Alta Road, Taos, NM 87571.
Tel: 505-758-8851;
http://www.nps.gov/rigr/

Snow melt from the Rocky Mtns. gives birth to the Rio Grande, the start of its 2,100-mi journey to the Gulf of Mexico. In northern New Mexico the river has cut a narrow **U-shaped gorge** through a thick layer of lavas that date back 2-4 million years, laid down when **fissure and shield volcanoes** erupted, spreading **lava** over the land. The crust beneath the **Rio Grande Rift Valley** has been slowly pulled apart for the past 25 million years. Take a river trip down the Rio Grande gorge to see the series of lava flows that have built the surrounding Taos Plateau. LCFRWB

ROCK ART RANCH

P. O. Box 224, Joseph City, AZ 86032. Tel. 928-288-3260; on Private Property - Phone Ahead - Reservations Required (Mon. - Sat. year-round).

One of the most significant **petroglyph sites** in the West. Ancestral Pueblo people (Anasazi) inscribed hundreds of symbols and representations of humans and wildlife on the walls of Chevelon Canyon in northeastern Arizona. Take a 4-mi trip across Painted Desert terrain to the canyon rim; it's then a 70-ft descent on stepping stones to the rock art panels below. The Baird family operates these tours and runs a cattle/buffalo ranch with a western museum; cowboy dinners served. Take I-40 Exit 252 to SR-87 south. Turn left on SR-99, then left on Territorial Rd. Look for sign to the ranch on right. CFRW

ROCK HOUND STATE PARK

P. O. Box 1064, Deming, NM 88031.
Tel: 505-546-6182;
http://www.emnrd.state.nm.us/nmparks/

A scenic place to camp (primitive and RV) and **collect mineral specimens** in the southwest corner of New Mexico. Unlike most parks, where prospecting or removing rocks is forbidden, this one was established for collectors. The easiest minerals to find are **quartz, perlite** (black volcanic glass with rounded pearly cracks), and several varieties of **jasper,** including **agate.** You might even discover an **opal.** It's a challenge to find prize specimens; come equipped with a large hammer, chisels, and a spade. Travelers may remove up to 15 pounds of rocks per visit. The park is not far from I-10, about 14 mi SE of Deming. CRWB

RUBY LAKE
NATIONAL WILDLIFE REFUGE

HC 60, Box 860, Ruby Valley, NV 89833.
Tel: 775-779-2237.

A blend of marsh, lake, and sagebrush habitats in a closed **Basin and Range** drainage system. Ruby Lake is one of two wetland remnants of a much larger ancient lake. The water comes from over **150 springs** at the base of the rugged and scenic Ruby Mtns. on the western edge of the refuge. Located 65 mi S of Elko. LFCRWB

SAGUARO NATIONAL PARK

Saguaro NP East: 3693 South Old Spanish Trail, Tucson, AZ 85730. Saguaro NP West: 2700 N. Kinney Rd., Tucson, AZ 85743. Tel: 520-733-5153 (East); 520-733-5158 (West); http://www.nps.gov/sagu/

Dedicated to preserving the giant saguaro cactus, King of the Sonoran Desert. The park is split into two sectors: East (Rincon Mtn. Unit, with a population of older saguaros) & West (Tucson Mtn. Unit, with a vigorous stand of younger plants). The city of Tucson sits in the drainage basin between these mountain ranges, typical **Basin & Range** topography. Saguaros thrive on the rocky **bajada** slopes that flank mountains in southern Arizona. Two 8-9 mi bajada loop drives and many hiking trails will quickly take you into this wondrous scenery. Ask at the Visitor Centers for information about the area's complex geology. And to see Hohokam **petroglyphs** inscribed on desert-varnished boulders, visit Signal Hill in Saguaro NP West, one of several fine picnic areas with shade ramadas. LFRWB

SALTON SEA
STATE RECREATION AREA

100-225 State Park Road, North Shore, CA 92254 Tel: 760-393-3052;
http://cal-parks.ca.gov/default.asp?page_id=639

In 1905, a broken agricultural dike flooded the Salton Trough, then a playa, creating an inland **salt lake** 35 mi long that is 228 ft below sea level. Tilted and crumpled rock formations show where the southernmost trace of the **San Andreas Fault** runs along the eastern edge of the lake; and at its southern end lie five small **lava domes** of rhyolite, the Salton Buttes. The lake has become an extremely important migratory stop for birds—about 400 species have been sighted here (see Strangest Lake in America, in Where Water Is). The Visitor Center is located 25 mi SE of Indio on SR-111. CFRWB

SAND MOUNTAIN RECREATION AREA

BLM, Carson City Field Office, 5665 Morgan Mill Road, Carson City, NV 89701. Tel: 775-885-6000; http://www.nv.blm.gov/carson/recreation/rec_sandmtn.htm

The quartz sand in this dune field (open to off-road vehicles) originated in Sierra Nevada granitic rocks eroded by glaciers 10,000+ years ago. The 600-ft-high deposit of sand is called "Singing Mountain" because, when conditions are right, the sand makes a booming or sighing sound as it slips down the face of the dune. The area is 25 mi SE of Fallon on US-50. CR (no W)B

SEDONA/ OAK CREEK CANYON

Sedona Chamber of Commerce, P.O. Box 478, Sedona, AZ 86339. Tel: 800-288-7336; http://dirs.educationamerica.net/cat/14438/ or http://www.publiclands.org/html/explore/stie.php?id=104

US-89A between Flagstaff and Sedona follows Oak Creek, which has cut deeply into the southern edge (the Mogollon Rim) of the **Colorado Plateau.** The creek is fed by **springs** that rise along the Oak Creek **Fault.** Red, iron-stained sandstone cliffs tower as much as 2,500 ft above the creek. Near Sedona—a jewel of a town set amongst red sandstone cliffs and monoliths—is Palatki **rock art** site with a sizeable **cliff dwelling** and the V-Bar-V Ranch Petroglyph Site; to visit either, contact the Sedona Ranger Station at 928-282-4119. LSFRWB

SHIPROCK

Farmington Chamber of Commerce, 203 Main St., Farmington, NM 87401. Tel: 800-448-1240.

This otherworldly landform is a **volcanic neck,** perhaps the most impressive one in the Southwest. Located 29 mi W of Farmington in northwestern New Mexico, US-64 passes north of the formation, but for a closer look at both the neck and its largest radiating **dike,** take US-666 S of the town of Shiprock for 6 mi and turn W on Indian Reservation Rd 13; 7 mi later the road meets the dike. This is a sacred landmark, so no climbing or camping is permitted. Head farther W to the Chuska Mtns. for the grand view of the valley and these volcanic features. F

SNOW CANYON STATE PARK

1002 N. Snow Canyon Dr., Ivins, UT 84738. Tel: 435-628-2255; http://www.stateparks.utah.gov/park_pages/scenicparkpage.php?id=scsp

A geological paradise of **lava flows, cinder cones,** and **sand dunes** exposed between red sandstone **mesas** and canyon walls painted with bluish-black **desert varnish.** Located 8 mi NW of St. George. There is a drive through the park along SR-8. LCFRW

SONORAN DESERT NATIONAL MONUMENT

Established Jan. 2001. BLM Phoenix Field Office, 21605 N. 7th Ave., Phoenix, AZ 85027. Tel: 623-580-5500; http://www.az.blm.gov/sonoran/sondes_main.htm or http://www.arizona.sierraclub.org/monuments

Situated 60 mi S of Phoenix, this new monument showcases dry and rugged desert mountains with scenic geological vistas. This is **Basin and Range** topography with three distinct mountain ranges and a diverse Sonoran Desert flora and fauna, along with many significant archaeological and historic sites. **Desert pavement** and **rock varnish** are well developed here;

Towering cliffs above the Virgin River Narrows, Zion National Park, UT.

and basalt-capped Table Top Mountain, with its 4,373-ft flat-topped summit, dominates the E end of the monument. Both I-8 and SR-238 cut through the monument just E of Gila Bend—for access, take I-8 Exit 119 and go S for about 5 mi; from Exit 140 or 144, go S (here the monument borders I-8). SR-238 (Maricopa Rd) offers access to the Maricopa Mountains and the Butterfield Overland Stage Route. Entry into the Sand Tank Mountains (Area A on some maps) by permit only. No facilities. 4-wheel drive recommended; no off-roading. LFBP (lodging in Gila Bend)

SP CRATER

(on private ranchland; your visit is a privilege—please don't abuse it). Inquire at Sunset Crater Volcano National Monument.

A classic **cinder cone** with its flow of **andesitic lava** in the San Francisco Volcanic Field. To get there, turn west on a small, unmarked dirt road (impassable when wet) that meets US-89 3 mi north of the turnoff to Wupatki National Monument. You'll see many cinder cones, and the road passes along the eastern edge of the main lava flow, which leads to SP Crater. No water, restrooms, or services; and no camping permitted.

SUNSET CRATER VOLCANO NATIONAL MONUMENT

Route 3, Box 149, Flagstaff, AZ 86004. Tel: 928-526-0502; http://www.nps.gov/sucr/

Visit the site of a recent volcanic eruption in the Southwest, Sunset Crater Volcano. This colorful **cinder cone**, one of over 600 in the San Francisco Volcanic Field, stands 1,000 ft above the surrounding plains. Cinders rich in oxidized iron and sulfur give the cone its permanent "sunset" glow. Vegetation is sparse, and the area appears to have cooled only a few decades ago; actually, the series of eruptions took place A.D. 1065-1250. Tour by car or hike the 1-mi self-guided loop trail though àà and pahoehoe **lava fields.** Sunset Crater Volcano's cinder cone is closed to hikers, but others in the vicinity are open to exploration. Please inquire at the Visitor Center. LCFRWB

TEXAS CANYON ROADSIDE REST AREA

Exit 318 on I-10 east of Benson, AZ

A one-hour drive east of Tucson, Texas Canyon cuts through the southern end of the Little Dragoon Mtns., exposing a wondrous area of rounded, granitic boulders that sport large pink feldspar crystals. Explore the **hoodoos** here, and note how weathering causes sheets of rock to peel off (exfoliate). The Butterfield Stage route once crossed this beautiful, rugged setting, also a backdrop for old western films. Other attractions in the area include the incredible **Amerind Foundation Museum** (www.amerind.org) of archaeology and **Cochise Stronghold** (www.cochisestronghold.com), a natural fortress that sheltered Apache Chief Cochise—supposedly buried here—and his people in the 1800s (access is by a rough dirt road with stream crossings; campsites available). LFRWB

TONTO NATIONAL MONUMENT

HC02, Box 4602, Roosevelt, AZ 85545. Tel: 928-467-2241; http://www.nps.gov/tont/

A park created to protect two 14th century Salado cliff dwellings nestled in natural limestone alcoves. The Salado farmed the Tonto Basin, part of the Salt River Valley that now holds Theodore Roosevelt Lake above Roosevelt Dam, the largest masonry dam in the world. These cliff dwellings were abandoned after little more than a century of occupation, and there's little agreement on why the Salado left or where they went. While in the area, don't miss the spectacularly scenic drive through Salt River Canyon south of the lake. LFRW

TONTO NATURAL BRIDGE STATE PARK

P. O. Box 1245, Payson, AZ 85547. Tel: 928-476-4202; http://www.pr.state.az.us/parkhtml/tonto.html

Believed to be the world's largest *travertine* bridge, located off SR-87, 13 mi NW of Payson. Calcium carbonate that formed this **natural bridge** came from the surrounding **limestone cliffs.** Visitors that venture up Pine Creek canyon will discover

springs and fern-lined **alcoves.** The park is restricted to day use only, and trails into the canyon are too steep and difficult for many people. LFRW

TOROWEAP OVERLOOK

Grand Canyon National Park, P.O. Box 8, Fredonia, AZ 86022. Tel: 928-638-7888, Ranger Station 928-638-7870; http://www.nps.gov/grca/

Spectacular views of Vulcan's Throne—a **cinder cone**—and **lava flows** that cascaded down the canyon walls. This remote spot on the North Rim of the canyon is only accessible by rough gravel roads, the shortest being a 70-mi stretch S of SR-389; to get there drive 9 mi W of Fredonia, turn onto Sunshine Rd at the "Toroweap" sign. This trip is not for the average traveler. A reliable, high clearance vehicle is essential; check with ranger for current conditions (tel: 520-638-7868). Take map and supplies; no water, food, or gas are available. From a nearby route, you can hike (extremely challenging and strenuous) down to Lava Falls on the Colorado R. CRB

TRONA PINNACLES

BLM, Ridgecrest Resource Area, 300 S. Richmond Rd., Ridgecrest, CA 93555. Tel: 760-384-5400; http://www.desertusa.com/Thingstodo/ttdtrails/du_ttd_trona.html/

More than 500 photogenic **tufa** spires dot the bed of Searles Dry Lake. Take SR-178 E from Ridgecrest for 27.7 mi; turn S on dirt road into site. The dirt access road is impassable after a rain. CB

VALLEY OF FIRES BLM RECREATION AREA

P.O. Box 515, Overton, NV 89040. Tel: 702-397-2088; http://www.publiclands.org/html/explore/stie.php?id=104

Only 30 mi NE of Las Vegas lies a surreal, undulating landscape of petrified dunes, weirdly shaped rocks, and brilliant red sandstone cliffs. The drive here from the south along SR-167 passes buckled, layered cliffs and desert plains. This is one of the most colorful locations in the Southwest, especially at sunset. From a distance the red rocks seem to be ablaze. **Petrified logs, tinajas,** and petroglyphs are just a few of the natural treasures to be discovered here. CFRWB

VALLEY OF FIRES
BLM RECREATION AREA

by U.S. 380 4 mi W. of Carrizozo, NM 88301. Tel: 505-648-2241; http://www.publiclands.org

According to Native American legend, the valley glowed with fires when Little Black Peak erupted and sent rivers of lava southward. This 44-mi lava flow is one of the world's longest; and the basalt here is about 5,000 years old and retains original surface textures. You can also see lava tubes, pressure ridges, blisters, and fissures. The campground is on a sandstone island known as a kipuka that pokes through the basalt flow. There's a Visitor Center, and the park's 1/3-mi, self-guided nature trail is handicap-accessible. LCFRWB

WALNUT CANYON
NATIONAL MONUMENT

Walnut Canyon Rd. #3, Flagstaff, AZ 86004. Tel: 928-526-3367; http://www.nps.gov/waca/

In Song of the Lark, Willa Cather set several crucial scenes in Walnut Canyon (called Panther Canyon in her novel). Here, over 800 years ago, a group known to archaeologists as the Sinagua built cliff dwellings in alcoves below limestone ledges. Two trails (one easy, one moderately strenuous) provide views of almost 100 rooms left vacant since about 1250, when these ancient people moved on. LFRW

WHITE SANDS
NATIONAL MONUMENT

P.O. Box 1086, Holloman AFB, NM 88330. Tel: 505-679-2599 or 505-479-6124; http://www.nps.gov/whsa/

Made famous by White Sands Missile Range nearby (where the first atomic bomb was tested in 1945), this Monument protects the largest gypsum dunefield in the world. In color and texture, the sand resembles refined sugar. It's a mystical and unforgettable landscape with something for everyone, adults and children alike. Guided nature tours are offered at sunset daily; and during summer months, you can enjoy nights by the light of a full moon. These dunes are so extensive, even photographers have no difficulty finding trackless expanses of sand not far from the road. A 4-mi loop trail will take you to a nearby alkali flat, a playa; and once a month, rangers lead a special tour to Lake Lucero, where mineral-laden water crystallizes into gypsum, the source of the sand—advanced reservations are required. LFRW+shaded picnic areas

VERMILION CLIFFS
NATIONAL MONUMENT

Established Nov. 2000. BLM Arizona Strip Field Office, 345 E. Riverside Dr., St. George, UT 84790. Tel.: 435-688-3246; http://www.az.blm.gov/vermilion/vermilion.htm

A new monument that includes the scenic Paria Canyon–Vermilion Cliffs Wilderness, bordering Kaibab National Forest to the west and Glen Canyon NRA to the east. A place of towering cliffs, swirling slickrock, and slot canyons. Vermilion Cliffs skirt the southern edge of the Paria Plateau, a spectacular 3,000-ft escarpment of colorful sandstone and shale. The area is rich in wildlife, and reintroduced California condors soar along the cliffs. Access from US-89 near milepost 26, S on House Rock Valley Rd or N from US-89A. 4-wheel drive essential for backcountry exploration. No facilities, except pit toilets at trail heads. Hiking permits required in Paria Canyon and Coyote Buttes areas—available online at www.az.blm.gov/paria/index2.html several months in advance or at the BLM Contact Station (open seasonally) near milepost 20 along US-89 W of Page. Avoid crushing the fragile fluted sandstone formations that abound here! LFRBP

WILCOX PLAYA

Willcox Chamber of Commerce, Willcox, AZ 86543. Tel: 800-200-2272; http://www.willcoxchamber.com

Nestled between the Chiricahua and Dragoon Mountains in southeastern Arizona is a great winter gathering ground for sandhill cranes. Contact the Chamber for information about the annual Wings over Willcox bird-ing festival in mid-January. Tour groups have special permission for access through private property. LFRW

ZION NATIONAL PARK

Superintendent, Springdale, UT 84767. Tel: 435-772-3256; http://www.nps.gov/zion/

Spectacular cliff and canyon landscapes carved in flat-lying strata of sandstones, mudstones, and limestones. Zion offers many hiking trails from easy 10-minute strolls to extended back country trips. A 15-mi round-trip hike will take you to world-famous Kolob Arch, large enough to span the length of a football field. The popular Gateway to the Narrows trail enters a stunning slot canyon, where the Virgin R. is a mere thread between smooth canyon walls that rise 2,000 ft to the plateau above. Wherever water seeps from the canyon walls, you'll find hanging gardens. And on the east side of the park, you'll see cross-bedded slickrock and the fractured layers of petrified dunes that form Checkerboard Mesa. LCFRWB

Good Books + Websites

An Annotated Selection

Abbey, Edward. 1968. *Desert Solitaire.* New York: Simon and Schuster. A famous novelist, poet, environmental activist, and visionary records his sojourn as a park ranger at Arches National Park, a best-seller that brought "canyon country" and Abbey to the world's attention.

Adams, Ansel. 1976. *Photographs of the Southwest.* Boston: Bulfinch Press. A regionally focused collection of inspiring black-and-white photographs by a photographer who needs no introduction.

Alden, Peter, and Peter Friederici. 1999. *National Audubon Field Guide to the Southwestern States.* New York: Alfred A. Knopf. A useful pocket natural history guide to AZ, NV, NM, and UT; includes a little bit of everything and 1,000 photos of common plants and animals for identification.

Annerino, John. 1999. *Canyoneering: How to Explore the Canyons of the Southwest.* Mechanisburg, PA: Stackpole Books. A useful paperback on the fundamentals of safe canyon exploration and the natural history of canyon country in the U.S. and Mexico. Nicely illustrated with black/white photos and drawings.

Austin, Mary. 1974. *Land of Little Rain.* (reprint from 1903). Albuquerque: Univ. of New Mexico Press. A poetic exploration of terrain, adaptation, and humanity in the deserts of AZ and southern CA—a literary classic in natural history writing.

Baars, Donald L. 1995. *Navajo Country—A Geology and Natural History of the Four Corners Region.* Albuquerque: Univ. of New Mexico Press. An in-depth treatment of Four Corners geology; black/white.

Barnes, F. A. 1978. *Canyon Country Geology for the Layman and Rockhound.* Salt Lake City: Wasatch Publishers. A good introductory text for the beginner, focused on SE Utah; black/white.

Bates, Robert L., and Julia Jackson, editors. 1997. *Dictionary of Geological Terms.* New York: Anchor Books, Doubleday. A useful reference prepared by the American Geological Institute.

Beck, Warren A., and Ynez D. Haase. 1989. *Historical Atlas of the American West.* Norman: Univ. of Oklahoma Press. Contains simple but useful maps showing locations of Indian tribes and reservations, Civil War sites, explorers' trails, wagon roads, and railroads, major mineral lodes, and catastrophic natural events. The maps are accompanied by easy-to read and informative explanations.

Bowers, Janice Emily. 1986. *Seasons of the Wind: A Naturalist's Look at the Plant Life of Southwestern Sand Dunes.* Flagstaff: Northland Press. A beautifully written overview of dune country, with detailed information on the largest and most frequently visited dunefields.

Cather, Willa. 1927. *Death Comes for the Archbishop.* Originally published by Alfred A. Knopf, now in various editions. One of Cather's best, this novel captured the history and flavor of northern New Mexico, including old Santa Fe and Albuquerque, the Little Colorado River, Laguna and Acoma Pueblos, and Hopi and Navajo settlements.

Childs, Craig. 2000. *The Secret Knowledge of Water: Discovering the Essence of the American Desert.* Seattle: Sasquatch Books. A travelogue, ecological treatise, and meditative essay— an informative, well-told story that's largely confined to Arizona.

Chronic, Halka. *Roadside Geology.* Missoula, MT: Mountain Press Publishing. An informative series of guidebooks to the geology of the Western states based on road logs. Black/white

——. 1988. *Pages of Stone: Geology of Western National Parks and Monuments.* Seattle: Mountaineers. A detailed, illustrated overview of geological features; mostly black/white.

Collier, Michael. 1999. *Water, Earth, and Sky—The Colorado River Basin.* Salt Lake City: Univ. of Utah Press. A beautiful collection of aerial photographs and essays.

Crampton, C. Gregory, editor. 1975. *Sharlot Hall on the Arizona Strip: A Diary of a Journey through Northern Arizona in 1911.* Flagstaff: Northland Press. Describes a woman historian's wagon trip through the Arizona territory north of the Grand Canyon after the turn of the century.

——. 2000 (first published in 1965 by Alfred A. Knopf). *Standing Up Country: The Canyonlands of Utah and Arizona.* Tucson: Rio Nuevo Press. A historian's look at the people and phenomena of canyon country; the new, edited-down edition is artfully illustrated with color photographs.

Crampton, Frank. 1993. *Deep Enough.* Norman: Univ. of Oklahoma Press. A graphic autobiography by a man who left the comforts of city life to embark on a career as a working stiff in western mining camps. Crampton explores all aspects of mining around the turn of the century in an engaging and humorous way.

Darwin, Charles and Ernst W. Mayr. 1975. *On the Origin of Species, a Facsimile of the First Edition.* Cambridge, MA: Harvard Univ. Press. Read this version of Darwin's revolutionary theory of evolution—considered the best—bundled with a stimulating introductory essay by preeminent biologist Ernst Mayr.

Duffield, Wendell A. and Michael Collier. 1997. *Volcanoes of Northern Arizona.* Grand Canyon, AZ: Grand Canyon Association. A concise, well-illustrated history of volcanoes of the Flagstaff area in particular—a fine, easy-to-understand reference for travelers and professionals alike.

Fillmore, Robert. 2000. *The Geology of the Parks, Monuments, and Wildlands of Southern Utah: A Geologic History with Road Logs of Highways and Major Backroads.* Salt Lake City: Univ. of Utah Press. Describes the geological processes that shaped the Colorado Plateau; includes entertaining notes on the history of the region and user-friendly road logs.

Hafen, Leroy R., and Ann W. Hafen. 1954. *Old Spanish Trail, Santa Fe to Los Angeles.* Glendale, CA (out-of-print). A readable history of one of the oldest trails in North America.

Harris, A.G., E. Tuttle and S. D. Tuttle. 1997. *Geology of National Parks, 5th edition.* Dubuque, IA: Kendall-Hunt Publishing. A detailed, illustrated overview that includes 12 of our Southwestern parks, a textbook approach; black/white.

Hartmann, William K. 1989. *Desert Heart: Chronicles of the Sonoran Desert.* Tucson: Fisher Books. An engaging, scholarly account of pioneers, geology, and archaeology of the Sonoran Desert region; superb photographs.

——, and Ron Miller. 1991. *The History of Earth—An Illustrated Chronicle of an Evolving Planet.* New York: Workman Publishing. A beautifully written synthesis of the geological and biological histories of our planet, with exquisite paintings and photographs by the authors.

Hillerman, Tony. A mystery series recognized by the Navajo Tribe for its faithful depiction of Navajo and Hopi life and culture; commands a good following among those who love the Southwest. Examples: *Fallen Man* (1997) focuses on Shiprock; *A Thief of Time* (1988) includes Anasazi history; *The Dark Wind* (1982) brings the Hopi mesas and traditions to life.

Iacopi, Robert L. 1996. *Earthquake Country.* Tucson: Fisher Books. Explains how, why, and where earthquakes strike in California.

Kappel-Smith, Diana. 1992. *Desert Time: A Journey Through the American Southwest.* Tucson: Univ. of Arizona Press. A perceptive, personal exploration of desert life and geology—enjoyable reading.

Klinck, Richard E. 1984. *Land of Room Enough and Time Enough.* Salt Lake City: Gibbs M. Smith, (out of print). A lively historical account of Monument Valley and the Navajo people.

Krutch, Joseph Wood. 1985 (reprint edition). *The Desert Year.* Tucson: Univ. of Arizona Press. A charming book by one of the Southwest's favorite natural history writers, straight-forward and enjoyable reading focused on the Sonoran Desert. No photographs.

Kuletz, Valerie. 1998. *The Tainted Desert: Environmental Ruin of the American West.* New York: Routledge. A sober historical review of uranium mining, weapons testing, and waste disposal in the Greater Southwest.

Lamar, Howard R., ed. 1998. *The New Encyclopedia of the American West.* New Haven, CT: Yale Univ. Press. Includes more than 2,400 alphabetized entries by 300+ contributors, covering every aspect of the history of the West, real and imaginary, in 1320 pages with over 600 illustrations. A thoroughly revised and expanded version of Lamar's 20-year-old Reader's Encyclopedia of the West. The type is extremely small.

Lamb, Simon, and David Sington. 1998. *Earth Story: The Shaping of Our World.* Princeton: Princeton University Press. A beautifully presented book with colorful photos and diagrams produced to accompany the BBC television series Earth Story.

Lambert, David. 1998. *The Field Guide to Geology.* New York: Facts on File. Concise handbook for beginners, with superb diagrams on every page.

Leach, Nicky J., and George Huey. 1992. *The Guide to National Parks of the Southwest.* Tucson: SW Parks and Monuments Assoc. A compilation of one-to-two-page descriptions of each federal park in AZ, NM, southern UT and CO, and west TX, with outstanding photos of each.

Martrès, Laurent R. 2002. *Photographing the Southwest.* Alta Loma, CA: Graphie Internat'l (PhotoTrip USA). Two very useful where-and-when guidebooks to natural landmarks of southern UT & southwestern CO (v. 1); AZ & NM (v. 2); black/white.

Matsen, Brad. 1994. *Planet Ocean—A Story of Life, the Sea, and Dancing to the Fossil Record.* Berkeley, CA: Ten Speed Press. An amusing and informative story about the evolution of life on Earth and the people who investigate it; illustrations are equally fun.

McPhee, John. 1981. *Basin and Range.* New York: The Noonday Press, Farrar, Straus and Giroux, 1981. McPhee, a 1999 Pulitzer Prize winner, captures the essence of geologic inquiry and translates it for non-scientists in an exploration of the land near and along Interstate 80; includes a lucid discussion of plate-tectonics.

McNamee, Gregory. 1994. *Gila: The Life and Death of an American River.* New York: Orion Books. A well-researched history of water, land, and public rights. The author received the Adult Author Award in 1995 from the Arizona Library Assoc. for this and other books.

Minch, John, Edwin Minch, Jason Minch, and John Minch. 1998. *Roadside Geology and Biology of Baja California.* Mission Viejo, CA: John Minch & Associates, Inc. A guide to the natural history of Baja, complete with kilometer-by-kilometer road logs to help travelers understand the scenery along major highways. Includes 194 photographs and 145 drawings.

Nabhan, Gary Paul, and Caroline Wilson. 1995. *Canyons of Color: Utah's Slickrock Wildlands.* New York: HarperCollinsWest. Illustrates in photographs and words the spectacular beauty, geologic history, and ecology of the slickrock country.

National Geographic's Guide to the State Parks of the United States. 1997. Washington, D.C.: Nat'l Geographic Society. Summarizes features, recreational opportunities, and contact information for more than 200 state parks.

Norman, David. 1985. *The Illustrated Encyclopedia of Dinosaurs.* New York: Crescent Books. Among the most informative and lavishly illustrated overviews on dinosaurs; includes behavior and other prehistoric reptiles too.

Norton, O. Richard. 1998. *Rocks from Space.* Missoula, MT: Mountain Press Publishing. Enjoyable and authoritative reading about meteorites, their origins, and the people who hunt and study them.

Patterson, Alex. 1992. *A Field Guide to Rock Art Symbols of the Greater Southwest.* Boulder, CO: Johnson Books. A fascinating cross-cultural classification of rock art symbols, for the novice and professional, with maps and directions to many important sites; black/white illustrations throughout.

Phillips, Steven J., and Patricia W. Comus, editors. 2000. *A Natural History of the Sonoran Desert.* Tucson: Arizona-Sonora Desert Museum Press; and Berkeley: Univ. of California Press. An excellent reference, largely written by museum and university scientists. This easy-to-digest compendium covers everything from desert soils to biodiversity, with about 2/3 of its 628 pp. devoted to descriptions of common plants and animals. Mostly black/white.

Powell, John Wesley. 1961. *The Exploration of the Colorado River and its Canyons.* Dover Publications. Powell merges his 1869 and 1871 descents of the Green and Colorado rivers into a colorful tale.

Price, L. Greer and Sandra Scott, editor. 1999. *An Introduction to Grand Canyon Geology.* Grand Canyon, AZ: The Grand Canyon Association. A concise, 64-page overview of geological processes and structural features of the West's most popular natural attraction, accompanied by dozens of illustrations and photographs.

Reisner, Marc. 1987. *Cadillac Desert: The American West and Its Disappearing Water.* New York: Penguin. A fact-filled story of how the misuse of Western water has wasted a once-beautiful landscape.

Sagan, Carl. 1980. *Cosmos.* New York: Ballantine Books. A scientific and philosophical overview of the universe and our place in it—a classic, rated the best-selling science book ever published in the English language.

Sharp, Robert P. 1994. *A Field Guide to Southern California.* Dubuque, IA: Kendall/Hunt. A geology book that introduces the basics and describes roadside geo-features; black/white.

——, and Allen F. Glazner. 1997. *Geology Underfoot in Death Valley and Owens Valley.* Missoula, MT: Mountain Press. A comprehensive, easy-to-read text on the geology of these great places; black/white.

Sherbrooke, Wade C. 2003 *Introduction to Horned Lizards of North America.* Berkeley: Univ. of California Press. A clearly written, well illustrated guide to the natural history of horned lizards, based on more than two decades of research by the author.

Steiert, Jim, and Wyman Meinzer. 1995. *Playas: Jewels of the Plains.* Lubbock: Texas Tech Univ. Press. An informative historical discussion of and guide to wetland ecology and playas in the High Plains of Texas. Richly illustrated with photographs.

Stokes, Wm. Lee. 1969. *Scenes from the Plateau Lands and How They Came to Be.* Salt Lake City: Starstone Publishing. A small, informative and friendly book about landforms of the Colorado Plateau; black/white.

Trimble, Stephen, and Terry Tempest Williams, editors.1996. *Testimony: Writers of the West Speak Out on Behalf of Utah Wilderness.* Minneapolis: Milkweed Editions. Essays by 21 of today's best nature writers on the urgent need to preserve wilderness areas.

Eyewitness Visual Dictionaries: The Visual Dictionary of the Earth (1998). New York: DK Publishing. A distinguished series of books for children and adults, packed with magnificent visuals and concise, informative text.

Waidhofer, Linde, and Lito Tejada-Flores. 1997. *Stone and Silence.* Sedona, AZ: Western Eye Press. A photographic exploration of sandstone landscapes in AZ, UT, and NM—winner of a Western U.S. Book Design Award for art/photography.

Waldman, Carl, editor. 1990. *Who Was Who in Native American History: Indians and Non-Indians from Early Contacts Through 1900.* New York: Facts on File. A compendium of 1,000 alphabetically arranged entries of famous and lesser-known figures in Indian history, ranging from Cochise to Davy Crockett. A good treatment, with no index and 50 poor photos.

Wild, Peter, editor, 1991. *The Desert Reader.* Salt Lake City: Univ. of Utah Press. The magic of the desert Southwest captured in words.

Wood, Charles A. and Jürgen Kienle, editors. 1993. *Volcanoes of North America: United States and Canada.* Cambridge Univ. Press (out of print). An excellent reference book—widely available in libraries—with succinct descriptions of 262 volcanoes and volcanic fields in 12 states and Canada. Much of the content is non-technical with photos, maps, and descriptions of how to find each volcano.

Zwinger, Ann. 1989. *The Mysterious Lands.* New York: Truman Talley Books/Plume. A noted naturalist explores the four great deserts of the American Southwest.

MORE WEBSITES

Excellent commercial **sites devoted to the Southwest,** both incredibly ambitious and well organized. Informative articles on geology, wildlife, places, and cultures. Book reviews, photographs, maps, weather, and wildflower updates as well.
http://www.desertusa.com
http://www.sidecanyon.com

Links from the Utah Geological Survey and the New Mexico Bureau of Mines & Mineral Resources to an enormous number of other **geologic web sites**—includes everything from science news to teaching resources to geologic associations.
http://www.ugs.state.ut.us/sites.htm
and http://geoinfo.nmt.edu/links.html

Valuable **links** to other websites featuring topics **of geological interest,** from the basics to specialties.
http://www-scf.usc.edu/~qobrien/

Websites of the **Hawiian Volcano Observatory,** packed with information, from earthquakes to eruptions and features a handy photoglossary of terms. http://hvo.wr.usgs.gov/volcanowatch and http://volcanoes.usgs.gov/Products/Pglossary

Website of the **USGS/Cascades Volcano Observatory**—includes maps and is not limited to the Cascades area. http://vulcan.wr.usgs.gov/Volcanoes

Authoritative information about **volcanoes** for kids and others, with a human touch.
http://volcano.und.nodak.edu

Valuable links to information about **volcanoes worldwide,** including current volcanic events.
http://users.bendnet.com/bjensen/links-volcano.html

Information on vertebrate **paleontology, esp. dinosaurs,** with a huge compendium of links to other sites.
http://www.isgs.uiuc.edu/dinos/dinos_home.html

Microsoft and Encarta maintain an extremely useful website featuring digitized **topographical maps and aerial photographs, including satellite images,** from the U.S. Geological Survey. Maps cover the U.S.A. in detail and can be downloaded for free.
http://terraserver-usa.com

A gateway to national **map products and services,** including everything from topo sheets to aerial photos and maps-on-demand.
http://mapping.usgs.gov/

A helpful guide to **public lands** in the West, with full information on recreational opportunities, fees, visitor facilities, books, and maps.
http://www.publiclands.org
http://www.recreation.gov

Visit Your National Parks, official website of the National Park Service that will take you to specific parks.
http://www.nps.gov/parks.html

A website on the **geology of our national parks** jointly created by the USGS and the National Park Service.
http://geology.wr.usgs.gov/

An easy-to-use directory to websites of U.S. **State Parks.**
http://www.ozarks.net/~outsider/parks/

Useful websites for information about **southwestern wetlands and birding hot-spots:**

• http://www.fws.gov/ for National Wildlife Refuges

• http://nature.org for Preserves of The Nature Conservancy

• http://thesierraweb.com/sightseeing/monolake.html for Mono Lake

• http://www.vtc.net/~seariz/cranes1.html for "Wings over Wilcox" annual Crane Celebration

A comprehensive guide to **recreational** opportunities and **rock art sites** under jurisdiction of the **Bureau of Land Managment in California.**
http://www.ca.blm.gov/caso/recreation.html

Photograph America Newsletter, packed with useful technical tips and information on where to go, when to go, and how to get there, in the Southwest and beyond. Go to http://www.photographamerica.com. for samples and subscription information.

A superb website about **Navajolands** prepared by a Navajo—includes cultural and historical perspectives, current events, and even information about landforms, complete with Navajo place names.
http://www.lapahie.com/

MINING MUSEUMS, TOURS + EXHIBITS

If you'd like to probe the pages of southwestern history or long for a close encounter of the mineral kind, explore these outstanding places:

ARIZONA

Arizona Rockhound & Tourist Information
For a statewide overview of rock collecting, gold panning areas, mine tours, and mineral museums and shows, visit http://www.admmr.state.az.us/rockhound.htm

Arizona Mining & Mineral Museum, Phoenix, AZ
An outstanding collection of minerals, with more than 3,000 on exhibit, including an 8-ft piece of native copper, moon rocks, fluorescent minerals, and a 206-lb fragment of Meteor Crater's meteorite. Also featured are a lapidary arts exhibit and an outdoor display of mining equipment. http://www.admmr.state.az.us/musgen.htm

Arizona-Sonora Desert Museum, Tucson, AZ
Most famous for its world-class exhibit of living plants and animals from the Sonoran Desert region, this museum also features a small but exceptional display of gems and minerals. http://www.desertmuseum.org

Bisbee, AZ
A semi-ghost town, now surviving as a quiet and quaint artist and retirement community. Of particular interest are the Bisbee Mining & Historic Museum and underground tours of the Queen Mine. http://www.bisbeearizona.com

Jerome, AZ
Another ghost town turned tourist town—not far from Sedona—with fascinating architecture and two great museums, the Jerome Historical Society Mine Museum and the Douglas Mansion/Jerome State Historical Park. http://www.jeromechamber.com/

Tombstone, AZ
A living ghost town, now designated as a National Historic Landmark; site of Tombstone Courthouse State Historic Park, Boothill Cemetery, saloons, folks in period costumes, gift-shops, and more—a theme-park atmosphere. http://www.tombstone.org

Tucson Gem, Mineral, & Fossil Show, AZ
The biggest buying, selling, and exhibition event of its kind in the world, held every February. Plan ahead—the show consumes the entire city for about three weeks. http://www.tucsonshowguide.com/

CALIFORNIA

Bodie State Historic Park, CA
One of the most interesting and best preserved ghost towns in the West, nestled in the hills north of Mono Lake. http://www.bodie.com

Natural History Museum of Los Angeles County, CA
The Mineral Science Hall houses one of the best gem and mineral exhibits in the world. http://www.nhm.org/sitemap/

COLORADO

National Mining Hall of Fame & Museum, Leadville, CO
Located in a famous 19th-century silver mining boomtown, the museum showcases the colorful history of mining in America. Leadville is in the Rocky Mtns., midway between Grand Junction and Denver, just south of I-70. http://leadville.com/miningmuseum/index.htm

NEVADA

Virginia City, NV
The largest federally designated Historical District in America, dedicated to preserving the character of this Old West mining town. Its Comstock Lode was the richest silver deposit ever found in the USA, which supported a booming population of 30,000 in the 1870s. With no less than nine museums, today's community of about 1,500 is devoted to tourism. http://museums.state.nm.us/nmmnh/nmmnh.html

NEW MEXICO

New Mexico Bureau of Mines & Mineral Resources Mineralogical Museum, Soccoro, NM

The best mining and mineral museum in the state, not far south of Albuquerque. http://geoinfo.nmt.edu/education/museum/home.html

New Mexico Museum of Natural History & Science, Albuquerque, NM
Among the best natural history museums in the Southwest; showcases dinosaurs along with minerals. http://www.nmmnhabq.mus.nm.us/nmmnh/exhibits.html

UTAH

Utah Museum of Natural History, Salt Lake City, UT

An older, small museum covering the geological and anthropological history of Utah with dinosaur skeletons, great displays of minerals from around the world, and a walk-in mine exhibit. http://www.umnh.utah.edu/

Index

Claret cup hedgehog cactus at Big Bend National Park, TX.

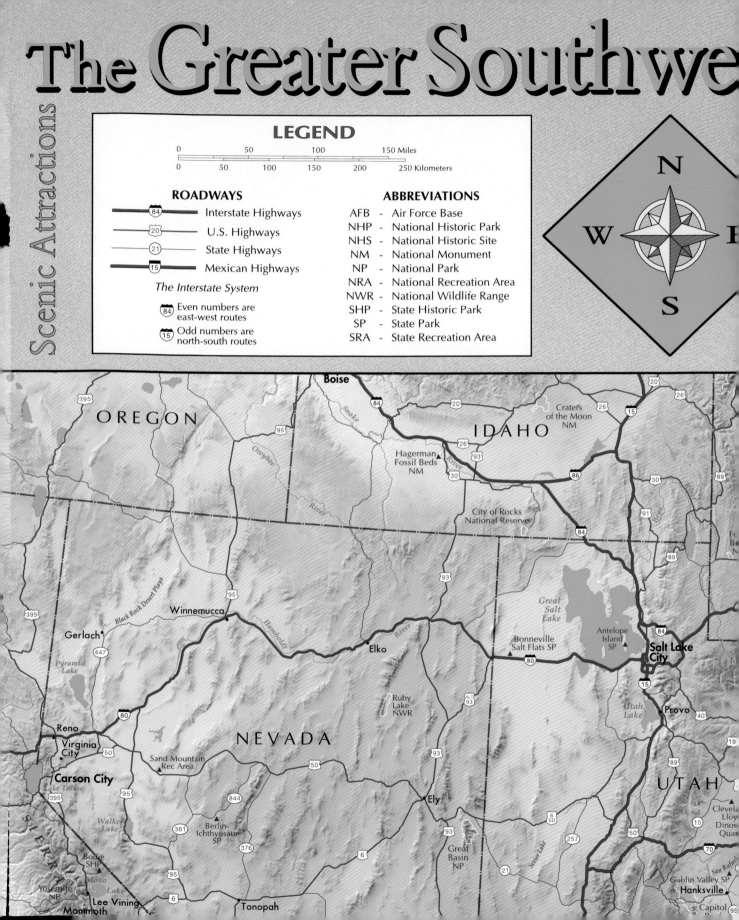

The Greater Southwe

LEGEND

0   50   100   150 Miles
0   50   100   150   200   250 Kilometers

ROADWAYS

Interstate Highways
U.S. Highways
State Highways
Mexican Highways

The Interstate System

Even numbers are east-west routes

Odd numbers are north-south routes

ABBREVIATIONS

AFB - Air Force Base
NHP - National Historic Park
NHS - National Historic Site
NM - National Monument
NP - National Park
NRA - National Recreation Area
NWR - National Wildlife Range
SHP - State Historic Park
SP - State Park
SRA - State Recreation Area

N W E S

OREGON

IDAHO

Boise

Craters of the Moon NM

Hagerman Fossil Beds NM

City of Rocks National Reserve

Snake River

Winnemucca

Gerlach

Black Rock Desert Playa

Pyramid Lake

Elko

Humboldt River

Great Salt Lake

Bonneville Salt Flats SP

Antelope Island SP

Salt Lake City

Reno

Virginia City

NEVADA

Ruby Lake NWR

Provo

Utah Lake

Carson City

Lake Tahoe

Sand Mountain Rec Area

Ely

UTAH

Walker Lake

Berlin-Ichthyosaur SP

Bodie SHP

Mono Lake

Great Basin NP

Sevier Lake

Goblin Valley SP

Hanksville

Cleveland Lloyd Dinosaur Quar

Yosemite NP

Lee Vining

Mammoth

Tonopah

Capitol

Fo Be

San Rafael

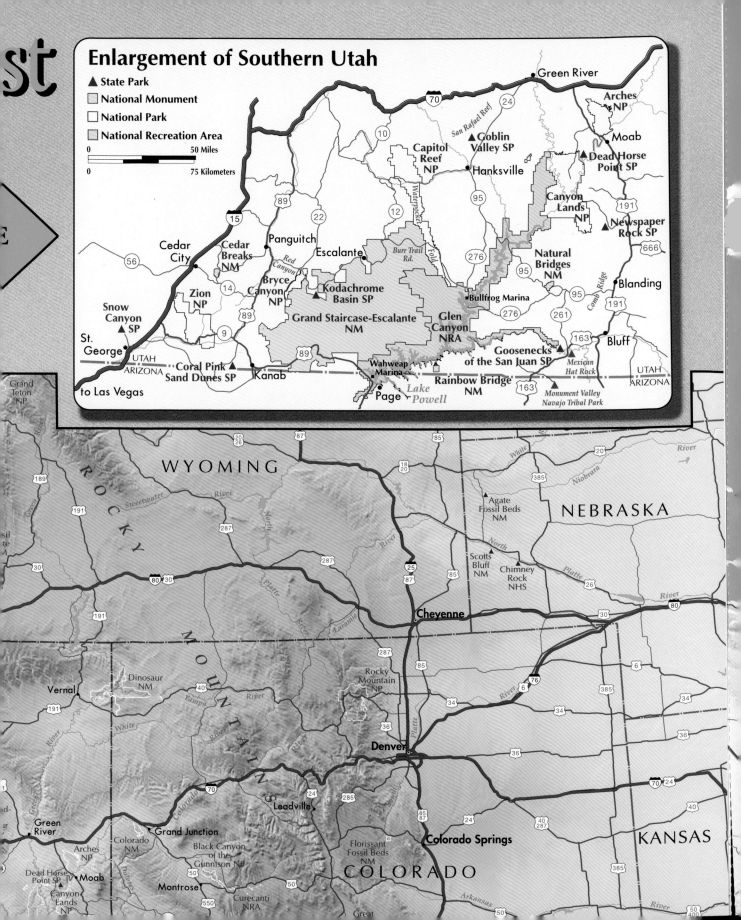

Enlargement of Southern Utah

▲ State Park
☐ National Monument
☐ National Park
☐ National Recreation Area

0   50 Miles
0   75 Kilometers

Green River

Arches NP

Moab

San Rafael Reef

▲ Goblin Valley SP

Capitol Reef NP

Hanksville

▲ Dead Horse Point SP

Canyon Lands NP

▲ Newspaper Rock SP

Cedar City

Cedar Breaks NM

Panguitch

Escalante

Red Canyon

Burr Trail Rd.

Waterpocket Fold

Natural Bridges NM

Blanding

Zion NP

Bryce Canyon NP

▲ Kodachrome Basin SP

Grand Staircase-Escalante NM

Glen Canyon NRA

Bullfrog Marina

Comb Ridge

Snow Canyon ▲ SP

St. George

UTAH
ARIZONA

Coral Pink ▲ Sand Dunes SP

Kanab

Wahweap Marina

Page

Lake Powell

Rainbow Bridge NM

▲ Goosenecks of the San Juan SP

Bluff

Mexican Hat Rock

▲ Monument Valley Navajo Tribal Park

UTAH
ARIZONA

to Las Vegas

WYOMING

Rocky

Sweetwater

Green

North

Platte

River

White

River

Niobrara

River

NEBRASKA

▲ Agate Fossil Beds NM

Scotts Bluff NM

Chimney Rock NHS

North Platte

Platte

River

Cheyenne

Laramie

River

Platte

River

Grand Teton NP

Dinosaur NM

Vernal

Yampa

River

White

River

Green

River

Mountains

Rocky Mountain NP

Denver

Platte

Leadville

Colorado

River

Green River

Grand Junction

Colorado NM

Black Canyon of the Gunnison NP

Florissant Fossil Beds NM

Colorado Springs

KANSAS

Arches NP

Dead Horse Point SP

Moab

Canyon Lands NP

Montrose

Curecanti NRA

COLORADO

Arkansas

River

Great